Great Italian Food
traditional and modern dishes

Great Italian Food
traditional and modern dishes

FALL RIVER PRESS

contents

special features

italian essentials

The characteristic simplicity of most Italian food is due to a few versatile, yet tasty, ingredients forming the basis of many delicious recipes. Following is a guide to those most widely used.

POLENTA
Polenta refers to both cornmeal and the dish made from it. Add dry polenta to boiling salted water or stock and stir until thick and smooth. Butter and parmesan can be added for extra flavor. Eat polenta as is, or pour into a baking dish, cool, cut into squares and grill or fry. Polenta makes a pleasant change from rice and mixes well with Mediterranean flavors and roasted meats or vegetables.

CIABATTA
Meaning 'slipper' in Italian, this flat, oval bread is slightly crunchy on the outside with a soft, chewy interior. The bread is light and porous and the flavor is delicately sour.

CIABATTA

FOCACCIA

FOCACCIA
This bread is usually made in a rectangular shape. It grills beautifully and is just the right thickness and texture for a grilled open sandwich. Cut the focaccia into a chunk, halve it, toast it lightly and pile on chopped salami, olives, sun-dried or fresh tomatoes, anchovies, sliced artichoke hearts and cheese. Grill for a few minutes to warm and melt the cheese, and you have the perfect lunch or snack.

PEPPERONI
A long, thin, Italian-style salami made with pork, beef and added fat. Pepperoni is seasoned with ground red pepper and is relatively spicy.

MORTADELLA
A soft-textured, smoked sausage with a mild flavor. Mortadella is made with pork fat, veal and beef, and flavored with spices and often pistachios.

MOZZARELLA
Mozzarella is a soft, elastic cheese, stretching into long strands when heated. It is used most often on pizzas, but can also be sliced and included in salads, or toasted in cheese sandwiches. It was originally made from buffalo milk, which can still be bought at specialty cheese shops, but it is now mostly made from cow milk.

Bocconcini are small balls of fresh mozzarella, stored in whey. They must be eaten within a day or two of purchase and refrigerated, covered, in a container of water. **Baby bocconcini** are tiny balls of bocconcini, and are lovely when halved and tossed into a salad.

PANCETTA
Pancetta has a distinctive red color, and it is one of the most popular cured meats. It comes from the flesh found directly under the skin around the pig's stomach. Each type of pancetta is prepared with salt and pepper, however some varieties also incorporate various spices.

PROSCIUTTO CRUDO
Sometimes called parma ham, this is a salted and air-cured ham, perfectly safe to eat raw. It is usually cut paper-thin and eaten with figs or slices of melon as a starter or part of an antipasto platter, but it can also be grilled or fried until crisp. Prosciutto cotto (cooked ham) is also available at some delicatessens.

PARMESAN
There are two types of Italian parmesan: Parmigiano Reggiano and Parmigiano Pedano. Reggiano is usually aged for three years, giving it a harder texture and a stronger, more mature flavor than Pedano. It also tends to be cheaper and more readily available. Parmesan is best bought in a block, and grated as required, as pre-grated parmesan quickly loses its flavor.

MOZZARELLA

PARMIGIANO REGGIANO

PARMIGIANO PEDANO

BOCCONCINI

BABY BOCCONCINI

ROMANO

PEPATO

PROVOLONE

CHEDDAR

SMOKED CHEDDAR

FONTINA

RICOTTA

GORGONZOLA

GOAT CHEESE

CREAM CHEESE

MASCARPONE

FETTA

to cook pasta

DRIED PASTA

Gradually add pasta to a large saucepan of boiling water, making sure water does not go off the boil. When cooking 'long' pastas, such as spaghetti, hold strands at one end until the submerged end becomes soft in the water. Gradually lower strands, coiling them neatly. Cook pasta until just tender; it should be 'al dente' (to the tooth) – tender but firm.

Cooking times for pasta will vary according to individual manufacturers so check pasta regularly to ensure it does not overcook.

Pasta should only be rinsed after draining if being used in a cold dish, or not being served immediately. In these cases, rinse pasta under cold running water to stop the cooking process, then drain.

Uncooked dried pasta can be stored up to a year in a cool, dry place. Cooked pasta can be refrigerated, covered, for 3 days.

FRESH PASTA

Fresh pasta is cooked in much the same way as dried pasta, however it requires much less cooking time.

Gradually add fresh pasta to a large saucepan of boiling water, making sure water does not go off the boil. Allow to cook for a few minutes until pasta is 'al dente'. It will not take long, so check pasta regularly to ensure it does not overcook.

WHY IS PASTA SO GOOD?

Pasta is usually made from wheat flour or semolina and water. It is a great source of carbohydrates and is fortified with folic acid, which may protect against certain cancers and heart disease. The complex carbohydrates give slow-release energy, making it popular amongst athletes and also good for diabetics. There is less than half a gram of fat in a ½-cup serving of pasta, so it is perfect for those watching their weight.

PASTA SHAPES

It is important to choose a pasta shape to complement your sauce. Generally, long, thin pastas suit light, thin sauces; thicker pastas suit heavier sauces; smaller shapes with ridges or holes are perfect for chunkier sauces; and small pastas, such as risoni and macaroni, are good in soups.

We have specified a pasta for each recipe, however if you prefer, simply substitute any pasta of your choice.

COME SI DICE?

Use this list of pronunciations to project your 'knowledge' of fine Italian cuisine:

amaretti *(am-ah-REHT-tee)*
antipasto *(ahn-tee-PAHS-toh)*
arborio rice *(ar-BOH-ree-oh)*
arrabbiata *(ar-rah-BEE-ah-tah)*
balsamico *(bal-SAH-mih-koh)*
biscotti *(bee-SKOH-tee)*
bocconcini *(bohk-KOHN-chee-nee)*
bruschetta *(broo-SKEH-tah)*
cacciatore *(kah-CHUH-tor-ee)*
calzone *(kal-ZOH-nay)*
cannoli *(kan-OH-lee)*
cappuccino *(kap-poo-CHEE-noh)*
carpaccio *(kahr-pah-CHEE-oh)*
conchiglie *(kon-KEEL-yeh)*
crostini *(kroh-STEE-nee)*
espresso *(ehs-PREHS-oh)*
fettuccine *(feh-TAH-chee-nee)*
focaccia *(foh-kah-CHEE-ah)*
gnocchi *(NYOH-kee)*
gorgonzola *(gohr-guhn-ZOH-lah)*
gremolata *(greh-moh-LAH-tah)*
lasagne *(luh-ZAHN-yuh)*
mascarpone *(mas-kahr-POH-nay)*
minestrone *(min-NES-TROHN-nay)*
mozzarella *(moht-SUH-REHL-lah)*
orecchiette *(oh-rayk-KEE-EHT-tay)*
osso buco *(AW-SOH BOO-koh)*
pancetta *(pan-CHEH-TUH)*
panforte *(pan-FOHR-tay)*
parmigiano *(pahr-MEE-jar-noh)*
penne *(PEN-nay)*
pepato *(peh-PAH-toh)*
pizza *(peet-ZUH)*
primavera *(PREE-mah VEHR-ah)*
prosciutto *(proh-SHOO-TOH)*
ricotta *(rih-KOH-TUH)*
saltimbocca *(sahl-TIHM-boh-KUH)*
tiramisu *(tih-ruh-mee-SOO)*
torrone *(toh-ROHN-nay)*
tortellini *(tohr-TL-EE-nee)*
vermicelli *(ver-ma-CHEL-ee)*
zabaglione *(zah-bahl-YOH-nay)*
zuccotto *(zoo-KOHT-toh)*
zuppa inglese *(zoo-PUH ihn-GLAY-zay)*

GREEN AND
YELLOW FETTUCCINE

SPAGHETTI

PAPPARDELLE

PENNE

CURLY
LASAGNE

RIGATONI

TAGLIATELLE

GREEN
AND WHITE
TORTELLINI

GOW GEE WRAPPERS

SMALL
SPIRALS

LASAGNE SHEETS

BOW TIES

antipasto

Traditionally served as an appetizer, a range of delicious antipasto is available, ready to serve, from large supermarkets or delicatessens. An appealing selection, as shown in this platter, should ideally include both purchased and homemade items, with as wide a range of tastes and textures as possible.

marinated olives with rosemary and thyme

tip oil will solidify on refrigeration; bring to room temperature before serving.

store recipe best made 3 days ahead; can be refrigerated for up to 3 months.

7oz green olives, drained
7oz black olives, drained
2 tablespoons fresh thyme
⅓ cup fresh rosemary
2 cloves garlic, sliced thinly
2½ cups (625ml) olive oil
½ cup (125ml) lemon juice

1 Layer olives, herbs and garlic into hot sterilized 4-cup jar.
2 Gently heat oil and juice in medium saucepan; do not boil. Pour enough of the oil mixture into jar to cover olives, leaving a ½-inch space between olives and top of jar; seal while hot.

preparation time 10 minutes (plus marinating time) cooking time 5 minutes makes 4 cups
per serving 17.3g fat; 173 cal

marinated eggplant

10 baby eggplants (1lb 5oz)
coarse cooking salt
4 cups white vinegar
2 cups (500ml) water
1 tablespoon coarsely chopped fresh mint

1 teaspoon dried thyme
1 clove garlic, sliced thinly
1 fresh red Thai chili, seeded, chopped finely
½ teaspoon ground black pepper
1½ cups (375ml) hot olive oil

store recipe best made 3 days ahead; can be refrigerated for up to 3 months.

1 Quarter eggplants lengthways; place in colander. Sprinkle with salt; stand 1 hour. Rinse eggplant under cold running water; drain on absorbent paper.
2 Heat vinegar, the water and 2 teaspoons of the salt in large saucepan until hot; do not boil.
3 Add eggplant; simmer, uncovered, 5 minutes. Drain; discard vinegar mixture.
4 Combine herbs, garlic, chilli, pepper and oil in large heatproof bowl.
5 Place eggplant upright in hot sterilized 4-cup jar. Carefully top with enough oil mixture to cover eggplant, leaving ½-in space between eggplant and top of jar; seal while hot.

preparation time 15 minutes (plus standing and marinating time) cooking time 10 minutes
makes 40 pieces per serving 2.8g fat; 30 cal

fennel vinaigrette

1½ cups (375ml) water
¾ cup (180ml) olive oil
¾ cup (180ml) white vinegar
¼ cup (60ml) dry white wine
1 medium brown onion (150g), sliced thinly
1 clove garlic, crushed
8 whole black peppercorns
1 bay leaf
1½ teaspoons yellow mustard seeds
4 medium fennel bulbs (4lbs 7oz)
1½ tablespoons coarsely chopped fresh fennel leaves

tip recipe can be
prepared 3 days ahead
and refrigerated, covered.

1 Combine the water, oil, vinegar, wine, onion, garlic, peppercorns, bay leaf and mustard seeds in large saucepan; bring to a boil. Reduce heat; simmer, uncovered, 4 minutes.
2 Trim tops from fennel bulbs; cut bulbs in half through center. Add fennel halves to vinegar mixture in saucepan; bring to a boil. Reduce heat; simmer, covered, about 15 minutes or until just tender.
3 Remove fennel from liquid, taking off any remaining particles from fennel. Strain liquid into large bowl; add fennel halves. Cool; stir in fennel leaves.
preparation time 10 minutes cooking time 25 minutes serves 4 per serving 41.4g fat; 455 cal

marinated mushrooms

¼ cup (60ml) lemon juice
½ cup (125ml) olive oil
¼ teaspoon salt

1 teaspoon finely chopped fresh tarragon
2 tablespoons finely chopped fresh parsley
9oz button mushrooms, sliced thinly

tip marinated mushrooms are delicious tossed through a green salad.

1   Combine juice, oil, salt, tarragon and parsley in medium glass or china bowl; mix well. Add mushrooms; mix well. Cover; marinate mixture 4 hours or overnight. [Can be made 2 days ahead to this stage.]
2   Using slotted spoon, remove mushrooms from marinade.
preparation time 15 minutes (plus marinating time) serves 4 per serving 28.7g fat; 270 cal

anchovy balls

2 cups (400g) medium-grain rice
2 teaspoons olive oil
3oz canned anchovy fillets in oil, drained,
    chopped finely
2 cloves garlic, crushed
2 tablespoons tomato paste
1 tablespoon finely chopped fresh parsley
2 tablespoons finely grated parmesan cheese
4½oz mozzarella cheese, cut into ½oz cubes
plain flour

2 eggs, beaten lightly
1 cup packaged breadcrumbs
vegetable oil, for deep-frying
tomato sauce
1 trimmed stick celery (3oz), chopped finely
1 small onion, chopped finely
1 clove garlic, crushed
½ cup (5oz) tomato paste
1½ cups (375ml) water

1   Cook rice in large saucepan of boiling water, uncovered, until just tender; drain.
2   Heat olive oil in small frying pan; cook anchovy, garlic, paste and parsley until fragrant. Combine rice and anchovy mixture in large bowl with parmesan. Mix well; cool.
3   Flatten a level tablespoon of the cooled rice mixture in one hand; top with a cube of mozzarella. Cover mozzarella with another level tablespoon of the rice mixture.
4   Carefully shape rice mixture into balls. Coat balls in flour; dip in egg, then breadcrumbs.
[Can be made a day ahead to this stage and refrigerated, covered.]
5   Heat vegetable oil in large saucepan; deep-fry balls, in batches, until golden brown. Drain on absorbent paper. Serve balls with tomato sauce.
tomato sauce cook celery, onion and garlic in heated small frying pan, stirring, until celery is soft. Stir in paste and the water; bring to a boil. Reduce heat; simmer, uncovered, about 15 minutes or until sauce thickens. [Can be made 2 days ahead and refrigerated, covered, or frozen for up to 3 months.]
preparation time 20 minutes (plus cooling time) cooking time 40 minutes serves 6
per serving 17.8g fat; 511 cal

seafood platter

1lb 2oz baby octopus
1lb 2oz medium uncooked shrimp
12 scallops
11oz calamari rings
11oz piece firm white boneless fish, chopped coarsely
11oz piece salmon
½ cup (125ml) olive oil
¼ cup (60ml) balsamic vinegar
¼ cup (35g) finely chopped, drained sun-dried tomatoes
2 tablespoons finely chopped fresh oregano
2 cloves garlic, crushed
1 tablespoon lime juice
3 uncooked lobsters (13oz), halved
12 small black mussels (9oz)

1 Remove and discard heads and beaks from octopus; cut each octopus into quarters. Shell and devein prawns, leaving tails intact.
2 Combine octopus, shrimp, scallops, calamari, fish and salmon in large glass or china bowl with oil, vinegar, tomato, oregano, garlic and juice; mix well. Cover; refrigerate 3 hours. [Can be made a day ahead to this stage.]
3 Remove octopus, scallops, calamari, fish and salmon from marinade. Cook, in batches, on heated oiled grill plate (or grill or barbecue), uncovered, until browned all over and just cooked through. Slice salmon.
4 Remove shrimp from marinade; discard marinade. Cook the shrimp and the lobster on grill plate until browned both sides and just changed in colour. Cook mussels on grill plate until shells open; remove and discard half of each shell.
5 Serve seafood on one large platter or individually.
preparation time 30 minutes (plus marinating time) cooking time 20 minutes serves 6
per serving 26.4g fat; 493 cal

bagna cauda

tip traditionally served warm, you can serve bagna cauda in a fondue pot with a small tea light or gentle flame underneath. Serve with your favourite selection of crisp vegetables.

2⅔ cups (600ml) thickened cream
2oz butter
2oz can anchovy fillets, drained, chopped finely
2 cloves garlic, crushed

1 Place cream in small saucepan; bring to a boil. Reduce heat to low; simmer, uncovered, about 15 minutes or until cream thickens, stirring frequently.
2 Meanwhile, melt butter over low heat in medium saucepan, taking care not to brown butter. Add anchovy and garlic; stir until mixture is blended well and becomes paste-like.
3 Stir hot cream into anchovy mixture until well combined; serve warm.
preparation time 5 minutes cooking time 20 minutes makes 2¾ cups per tablespoon 9.5g fat; 88 cal

little fried cheese pastries

1½ cups flour
½ cup self-raising flour
1 tablespoon olive oil
¾ cup (180ml) beef stock
¼ cup ricotta cheese
⅓ cup grated smoked cheddar cheese
½ cup grated mozzarella cheese

⅓ cup grated parmesan cheese
2oz thinly sliced salami, chopped finely
1 egg white, beaten lightly
1 tablespoon finely chopped fresh rosemary
pinch ground nutmeg
vegetable oil for deep-frying

1 Sift flours into large bowl; make well in center. Pour in a small amount of combined olive oil and stock. Using one hand, work in flour a little at a time. Gradually add stock mixture, working in flour until mixture comes together in a ball.
2 Press mixture together to give a firm dough. Knead dough on lightly floured surface about 5 minutes or until dough is smooth and elastic. Cover dough with slightly damp cloth; stand 5 minutes.
3 Meanwhile, combine cheeses, salami, egg white, rosemary and nutmeg in medium bowl; mix well.
4 Roll dough on lightly floured surface until as thin as possible. Cut into 2in rounds. Cover with slightly damp cloth to prevent dough drying out.
5 Place 1 level teaspoon of the cheese mixture in centre of each round. Brush edges of rounds with a little water. Place another round on top of cheese mixture; press edges together firmly.
6 Heat vegetable oil in large saucepan; deep-fry pastries, in batches, until browned. Drain on absorbent paper.
preparation time 30 minutes (plus standing time) cooking time 35 minutes makes 45
per pastry 2.6g fat; 50 cal

marinated calamari

1lb 2oz calamari rings
⅓ cup (80ml) lemon juice
⅓ cup (80ml) olive oil
1 clove garlic, crushed
1 tablespoon finely chopped fresh parsley

store recipe can be made 2 days ahead and refrigerated, covered.

1 Drop calamari into large saucepan of rapidly boiling water; reduce heat. Simmer about 10 minutes, or until calamari is tender; drain. Combine juice and oil in medium glass or china bowl; add calamari. Cover; refrigerate overnight. [Can be made a day ahead to this stage.]
2 Add garlic and parsley to marinade; mix well. Let stand 2 hours or longer in marinade; serve calamari in marinade.
preparation time 25 minutes (plus refrigerating and marinating time) cooking time 15 minutes serves 4
per serving 19.3g fat; 235 cal

roasted tomatoes with garlic and herbs

store recipe can be made 3 days ahead and refrigerated, covered.

9 large tomatoes (2lbs 11oz), halved

1 tablespoon extra virgin olive oil

1 teaspoon sea salt

1 teaspoon cracked black pepper

8 sprigs fresh thyme

2 cloves garlic, peeled, sliced thinly

2 teaspoons finely chopped fresh oregano

1 teaspoon finely chopped fresh thyme, extra

2 tablespoons extra virgin olive oil, extra

1 Place tomatoes in large baking dish with oil, salt, pepper, thyme and garlic.

2 Bake in moderately hot oven about 1 hour or until tender and browned lightly.

3 Drizzle with combined oregano, extra thyme and extra oil. serve warm or cold.

preparation time 10 minutes cooking time 1 hour serves 6 per serving 9.3g fat; 107 cal

beans with tomato

1oz butter

1 clove garlic, crushed

2oz can anchovy fillets, drained, chopped finely

2 medium onions, chopped finely

3 medium tomatoes (1lb 4oz), chopped finely

1 tablespoon tomato paste

2 teaspoons finely chopped fresh basil

½ teaspoon sugar

2lbs 4oz borlotti beans, shelled

1 cup (250ml) water

2 teaspoons finely shredded fresh basil, extra

tips 1lb 4oz canned borlotti or cannellini beans can be substituted for the shelled borlotti beans; rinse and drain beans before adding for last 10 minutes of cooking. Recipe can be made 2 days ahead and refrigerated, covered; reheat or bring to room temperature before serving.

1 Melt butter in large saucepan; cook garlic, anchovy, onion and tomato until onion is transparent. Add paste, basil, sugar and beans; mix until well combined.

2 Add the water; bring to a boil. Reduce heat; simmer, covered, about 30 minutes or until beans are tender. Stir through extra basil.

preparation time 35 minutes cooking time 40 minutes serves 6 per serving 8.2g fat; 495 cal

carpaccio with fresh herbs

1lb piece of beef eye-fillet, about 2½in diameter
⅓ cup (80ml) extra virgin olive oil
¼ cup (60ml) lemon juice
¼ cup firmly packed fresh basil
¼ cup firmly packed fresh flat-leaf parsley
1 tablespoon fresh oregano
1 tablespoon coarsely chopped fresh chives
¼ cup (25g) drained sun-dried tomatoes, sliced thinly
2 tablespoons flaked parmesan cheese
freshly ground black pepper

tips sashimi-quality tuna can be used in place of the beef; ask the fishmonger to slice tuna, paper-thin, for you.
Omit the parmesan and add a sprinkling of baby capers.

1 Remove any excess fat from beef. Wrap beef tightly in plastic wrap; freeze about 1½ hours or until partly frozen.
2 Cut beef into paper thin slices; freeze until required. [Store in freezer container, between layers of freezer wrap, for up to 2 months.]
3 Just before serving, place beef on serving plate. Drizzle with oil and juice; top with combined herbs, tomato, cheese and pepper.
preparation time 25 minutes (plus freezing time) serves 8 per serving 129g fat; 178 cal

pesto dip with crisp garlic wedges

1 cup firmly packed, coarsely chopped
   fresh basil
1 clove garlic, crushed
2 tablespoons pine nuts, toasted
2 tablespoons finely grated fresh
   parmesan cheese
2 tablespoons olive oil
2 teaspoons lemon juice
1¼ cups sour cream

crisp garlic wedges
4 pita
5oz butter, melted
2 cloves garlic, crushed
⅔ cup finely grated fresh
   parmesan cheese

1 Blend or process basil, garlic, pine nuts, cheese, oil and juice until smooth. Combine in medium
bowl with sour cream.
2 Serve with crisp garlic wedges. [Can be made a day ahead and refrigerated, covered.]
crisp garlic wedges split pita in half; cut into large wedges. Place split-side up on oven trays. Brush
with combined butter and garlic; sprinkle with cheese. Bake at 350º F for about 8 minutes or until browned
lightly and crisp. [Can be made a week ahead and stored in airtight container or frozen
for up to 2 months.]
preparation time 10 minutes cooking time 25 minutes serves 6 per serving 54.5g fat; 642 cal

baked mushrooms

9 medium cap mushrooms
2oz butter, melted
3 bacon slices, chopped finely
4 green onions, chopped finely
2 cloves garlic, crushed

2 tablespoons stale breadcrumbs
1 tablespoon cream
2 teaspoons fresh oregano, chopped coarsely
2 tablespoons grated parmesan cheese

1 Gently remove stalks from eight of the mushrooms. Finely chop stalks and remaining mushroom.
2 Brush mushroom caps all over with butter. Place on lightly greased cookie sheet.
3 Cook bacon and onion in small frying pan until bacon is crisp. Add chopped mushroom, garlic
and breadcrumbs. Cook, stirring, until well combined. Remove from heat; stir in cream, oregano and
cheese. Divide bacon mixture between mushroom caps. [Can be made 3 hours ahead to this stage
and refrigerated, covered.]
4 Bake in moderately hot oven about 10 minutes or until hot.
preparation time 15 minutes cooking time 10 minutes serves 4 per serving 17.4g fat; 236 cal

deep-fried sardines

1 cup flour
¼ cup coarsely chopped fresh basil
1 teaspoon garlic salt
1lb 2oz sardines
vegetable oil, for deep-frying
spiced mayonnaise dip
1 cup mayonnaise
2 cloves garlic, crushed
2 tablespoons lemon juice
1 tablespoon drained capers, chopped finely
1 tablespoon coarsely chopped fresh flat-leaf parsley

tip serve as a starter, or present on a platter as finger food for a party.

1 Combine flour, basil and garlic salt in large bowl. Toss sardines in flour mixture, in batches, until coated.
2 Heat oil in medium saucepan. Deep-fry sardines, in batches, until browned and cooked through; drain on absorbent paper. Serve with spiced mayonnaise dip.
spiced mayonnaise dip combine mayonnaise, garlic, juice, capers and parsley in small serving bowl.
preparation time 10 minutes cooking time 15 minutes serves 4 per serving 48.1g fat; 706 cal

baked mussels

24 small black mussels (1lb 2oz)
¾ cup (180ml) water
¼ cup (60ml) olive oil
1 clove garlic, crushed

2 tablespoons finely chopped fresh parsley
½ cup stale breadcrumbs
1 medium tomato (5oz), seeded,
   chopped finely

1 Scrub mussels, remove beards. Heat the water in large saucepan. Cook mussels in the water, covered, over high heat about 3 minutes or until shells open. Drain; discard liquid.
2 Loosen mussels; remove from shell. Discard half of each shell, reserve half. Combine mussel meat, oil, garlic, parsley and breadcrumbs in small bowl; mix well. Cover; refrigerate 30 minutes. [Can be made a day ahead to this stage.]
3 Place one mussel in each half shell; place on oven tray. Combine tomato with remaining breadcrumb mixture; spoon over mussels. Bake in hot oven about 5 minutes or until breadcrumbs are browned lightly.
preparation time 20 minutes (plus marinating time) cooking time 10 minutes serves 4
per serving 14.5g fat; 176 cal

marinated artichoke hearts

10 medium globe artichokes (4lbs 7oz)
3 medium lemons, halved
1 clove garlic, crushed
1 teaspoon black peppercorns

4 cups white vinegar
2 cups water
1½ cups hot olive oil, approximately

store recipe can be made 3 months ahead and refrigerated.

1 Cut stems from artichokes. Snap off tough outer leaves until you are left with a central cone of leaves.
2 Trim away any dark green parts; cut away top of cones. Rub artichokes all over with a lemon half. Place artichokes in large glass or china bowl with another lemon half; cover well with water.
3 Heat combined garlic, peppercorns, vinegar and the water in large non-reactive saucepan until hot; do not boil. Add drained artichokes and remaining lemons; simmer, uncovered, 15 minutes or until chokes are easy to remove from centres. Drain; cool 5 minutes.
4 Remove and discard center leaves and chokes using a small spoon. Cut artichoke hearts in half; place hearts in sterilized 4-cup jar. Top with enough oil to cover, taking care as it will bubble. Leave a ½-in space between hearts and top of jar; seal while hot. Refrigerate 1 week before using.
preparation time 30 minutes (plus marinating and standing time) cooking time 20 minutes
serves 8 per serving 7.3g fat; 106 cal

olives

black olive paste

Blend or process 4 cloves chopped garlic, 4 cups seeded black olives, 5 drained anchovy fillets, 1 tablespoon drained capers, ½ cup coarsely chopped fresh parsley and 1 tablespoon coarsely chopped fresh oregano until chopped finely. Gradually add 1 cup extra virgin olive oil, in a thin stream, while motor is operating; process until smooth. Spoon into hot sterilized jar. Cover with a thin layer of oil; seal.

preparation time 15 minutes makes 3½ cups
per tablespoon 8.3g fat; 85 cal

store paste can be refrigerated 3 weeks.

olives in cheese pastry

Sift 1 cup flour into a medium bowl; rub in 4oz coarsely chopped butter. Stir in 1 cup finely grated parmesan cheese and 2 teaspoons dried oregano; add up to 2 tablespoons water until ingredients cling together. Cover; refrigerate 30 minutes. Drain 50 small stuffed olives on absorbent paper. Roll pastry between sheets of greaseproof paper until ⅛in thick; cut 1½in rounds from pastry. Top each round with an olive; fold pastry around olive to enclose. Place olives ¼in apart on greased oven trays. Cover; refrigerate 30 minutes. [Can be made a day ahead to this stage.] Bake, uncovered, in moderately hot oven about 20 minutes or until golden; cool.

preparation time 35 minutes (plus refrigeration time) cooking time 20 minutes makes 50
per pastry 3.2g fat; 37 cal

tip pastry for wrapping olives is best rolled only once for the wrapping process – more rolling causes it to shrink on cooking.

store recipe can be made a day ahead and stored in airtight container. Can be frozen, uncooked, for up to 3 months.

garlic chili black olives

Place 1lb 11oz drained black olives in hot sterilized 5-cup jar. Gently heat 2 cups olive oil, ⅓ cup balsamic vinegar, 6 dried red Thai chilies, 4 halved garlic cloves and 3 strips lemon rind in small saucepan until warm. Pour enough of the oil mixture into jar to cover olives completely, leaving ¼in space between olives and top of jar; seal while hot.

preparation time 10 minutes (plus standing time)
cooking time 5 minutes makes 5 cups
per tablespoon 2.5g fat; 36 cal

store recipe best made 3 days ahead; can be refrigerated 3 weeks.

orange and oregano marinated green olives

Layer 1¼lb large, drained green olives, 3 orange slices cut into quarters and 5 sprigs fresh oregano into hot sterilized 4-cup jar. Gently heat 1 cup olive oil, ½ cup orange juice and 2 teaspoons whole black pepper in small saucepan. Pour enough of the oil mixture into jar to cover olives completely, leaving ¼in space between olives and top of jar; seal while hot.

preparation time 10 minutes (plus standing time)
cooking time 5 minutes makes 4 cups
per tablespoon 2.9g fat; 34 cal

tip oil will solidify on refrigeration; bring to room temperature before serving.

store recipe best made 3 days ahead; can be refrigerated 3 weeks.

soup

Hearty is probably the best word to describe Italian soups. Rich with a variety of vegetables, or fragrant with the abundant fresh seafood of the Mediterranean, finished with a sprinkling of grated parmesan or freshly chopped herbs, these soups can often serve as meals in themselves. Just add crusty bread and a simple salad.

rocket and pancetta soup

4oz thinly sliced pancetta

1 tablespoon olive oil

1 medium red onion, chopped coarsely

2 cloves garlic, quartered

1½ tablespoons balsamic vinegar

4 medium potatoes, chopped coarsely

3 cups (750ml) chicken stock

3 cups (750ml) water

1lb 2oz rocket, trimmed

¼ cup finely grated parmesan cheese

tip prosciutto can be substituted for the pancetta.

1 Place pancetta in single layer on oven tray. Bake, uncovered, in moderate oven, about 15 minutes or until crisp. Drain pancetta on absorbent paper; chop coarsely.

2 Heat oil in large saucepan; cook onion and garlic, stirring, until onion softens. Add vinegar and potato; cook, stirring, 5 minutes.

3 Add stock and the water; bring to a boil. Reduce heat; simmer, uncovered, about 15 minutes or until potato softens. Stir in rocket; cook, stirring, about 2 minutes or until rocket wilts.

4 Blend or process soup mixture, in batches, until smooth. Return soup to cleaned saucepan; stir over heat until hot. Divide soup among serving bowls; sprinkle with cheese and pancetta.

preparation time 20 minutes cooking time 35 minutes serves 6 per serving 7g fat; 204 cal

stracciatella

5 eggs

½ cup finely grated parmesan cheese

6 cups chicken stock

2 tablespoons finely chopped fresh
    flat-leaf parsley

ground nutmeg

tips break eggs one at a time into a small cup before adding to the recipe; this way, if one egg is bad, you can discard it.
Make sure you add the egg and cheese mixture gradually or you will end up with large clumps of 'scrambled' egg.

1 Lightly whisk eggs with cheese in medium jug until combined.

2 Bring stock to a boil in large saucepan. Remove from heat; gradually add egg mixture, whisking constantly.

3 Return mixture to heat; simmer, stirring constantly, about 5 minutes or until egg mixture forms fine shreds. Stir in parsley; sprinkle with nutmeg.

preparation time 5 minutes cooking time 10 minutes serves 6 per serving 6.9g fat; 144 cal

seafood soup with gremolata

4lbs 7oz fish bones
1 medium onion, chopped coarsely
1 medium carrot, chopped coarsely
2 trimmed sticks celery, chopped coarsely
16 cups water
8 black peppercorns
2 bay leaves
1 tablespoon olive oil
1 medium onion, chopped coarsely, extra
2 cloves garlic, crushed
5 medium tomatoes (2lbs 2oz), chopped finely
3 teaspoons sugar
14oz canned tomatoes
¼ cup tomato paste

½ cup (125ml) dry white wine
2 medium uncooked lobster tails (1lb 11oz),
    shelled, chopped coarsely
14oz boneless firm white fish fillets,
    chopped coarsely
gremolata
1 clove garlic, chopped finely
1 tablespoon finely chopped lemon rind
2 tablespoons finely chopped fresh
    flat-leaf parsley

tip shrimp or crabs can be substituted for the lobster.

1 Combine fish bones, onion, carrot, celery, the water, peppercorns and bay leaves in large saucepan. Simmer, uncovered, 20 minutes. Strain stock over large bowl; discard bones, vegetables and seasonings. [Can be made a day ahead to this stage and refrigerated, covered, or frozen for up to 2 months.]
2 Heat oil in large saucepan; cook extra onion and garlic, stirring, until onion softens. Add tomato and sugar; cook, stirring, about 10 minutes or until tomato is soft. Stir in undrained crushed tomatoes, paste and wine; bring to a boil. Reduce heat; simmer, uncovered, about 5 minutes or until mixture thickens slightly, stirring occasionally. Add stock; bring to a boil. Reduce heat; simmer, uncovered, 20 minutes. Cool 10 minutes.
3 Blend or process tomato mixture, in batches, until pureed; return to cleaned saucepan. Bring to a boil; add lobster and fish. Reduce heat; simmer, stirring, about 5 minutes or until seafood is just cooked.
4 Divide soup among serving bowls; sprinkle each with gremolata.
gremolata combine ingredients in small bowl.
preparation time 30 minutes cooking time 1 hour 20 minutes serves 6 per serving 6.6g fat; 293 cal

lentil soup

¼ cup (60ml) olive oil

1 large onion (7oz), chopped coarsely

1 medium eggplant (11oz), quartered

4 medium tomatoes (1lb 11oz), quartered

1 large red pepper, quartered

3 cloves garlic, peeled

8 cups vegetable stock

1 cup puy lentils

½ cup (125ml) sour cream

2 tablespoons finely chopped fresh chives

tip brown lentils can be substituted for the puy lentils, although they do require longer cooking.

1 Combine oil, onion, eggplant, tomato, pepper and garlic in large baking dish. Bake, uncovered, in hot oven about 45 minutes or until vegetables are tender. Turn once halfway through cooking.

2 Place pepper pieces on plate, skin-side up. Cover; stand 5 minutes. Peel pepper, tomato and eggplant; discard skin. Chop flesh coarsely keeping each vegetable separate.

3 Blend or process eggplant with garlic and onion until pureed; combine with stock and lentils in large saucepan. Bring to a boil; reduce heat; simmer, uncovered, about 35 minutes or until lentils are tender. [Can be made a day ahead to this stage and refrigerated, covered.]

4 Add pepper and tomato; stir over heat until hot. Divide soup among serving bowls. Dollop each with sour cream; sprinkle with chives.

preparation time 15 minutes cooking time 1 hour 25 minutes serves 6 per serving 19.2g fat; 335 cal

minestrone

½ cup dried cannellini beans

2 teaspoons olive oil

1 medium onion (5oz), chopped finely

2 cloves garlic, crushed

10 slices prosciutto, chopped coarsely

1 trimmed stick celery, chopped finely

1 medium carrot, chopped finely

1 medium green zucchini, chopped finely

1lb 13oz canned tomatoes

6 cups chicken stock

1 medium potato, chopped finely

1 cup ditalini

1 cup loosely packed finely shredded savoy cabbage

1 cup loosely packed, finely shredded spinach leaves

1 tablespoon finely shredded fresh basil

½ cup grated parmesan cheese

tips macaroni or any small tubular pasta can be substituted for the ditalini. Make basic soup mixture (up to and including step 3) when you soak the beans (ie, the day before required), to allow the flavors to develop. Top each bowl of soup with a teaspoon of basil pesto, to make minestrone genovese.

1 Place beans in medium bowl; cover with water. Stand overnight; drain.

2 Heat oil in large saucepan; cook onion and garlic, stirring, until onion is soft. Add prosciutto, celery, carrot and zucchini; cook, stirring, 5 minutes. Stir in undrained crushed tomatoes and stock; bring to a boil. Reduce heat; simmer, uncovered, 30 minutes.

3 Stir in beans and potato; simmer, uncovered, 15 minutes. [Can be made a day ahead to this stage and refrigerated, covered, or frozen for up to 3 months.]

4 Add pasta; simmer, uncovered, about 10 minutes or until pasta is tender.

5 Just before serving, stir in cabbage, spinach and basil; serve soup sprinkled with cheese.

preparation time 25 minutes (plus soaking time) cooking time 1 hour 10 minutes serves 6
per serving 8.7g fat; 350 cal

tuscan bean soup

1½ cups dried haricot beans
1 tablespoon olive oil
1 medium onion, chopped coarsely
2 cloves garlic, crushed
2 trimmed sticks celery, chopped coarsely
1 medium carrot, chopped coarsely
2 bacon slices, chopped coarsely

4 large ripe tomatoes (2lbs 4oz), peeled, chopped coarsely
6 cups vegetable stock
1 teaspoon sugar
¼ cup fresh parsley sprigs
¼ cup tomato paste

1 Cover beans with water in large bowl; stand, covered, overnight.
2 Heat oil in large saucepan; cook onion, garlic, celery, carrot and bacon, stirring, until vegetables are just tender.
3 Add tomato; cook, stirring, about 5 minutes or until tomato is soft.
4 Stir in rinsed drained beans, stock, sugar, parsley and paste; bring to a boil. Reduce heat; simmer, covered, about 1½ hours or until beans are tender. [Can be made a day ahead and refrigerated, covered or frozen for up to 2 months.]
preparation time 25 minutes (plus soaking and standing time) cooking time 1 hour 40 minutes
serves 4 per serving 16.8g fat; 729 cal

bread

onion focaccia

Sift 2½ cups flour into large bowl; stir in 2 teaspoons dry yeast, ¼ cup grated parmesan cheese, 2 tablespoons coarsely chopped fresh sage and 1 teaspoon sea salt. Gradually stir in 1 cup warm water and 2 tablespoons olive oil. Knead on well floured surface 10 minutes or until smooth and elastic. Place on greased oven tray; press into a 9½-in round. Cover with greased plastic wrap; stand in warm place until doubled in size. Meanwhile, combine 1 small thinly sliced white onion, 2 teaspoons sea salt and 1 tablespoon olive oil in small bowl; sprinkle mixture over dough. Bake in hot oven 25 minutes or until cooked when tested; cool on wire rack.
preparation time 20 minutes (plus standing time)
cooking time 25 minutes (plus cooling time)
serves 8 per serving 8.2g fat; 238 cal

olive bread with oregano

Combine 1 tablespoon dry yeast, 1 teaspoon sugar and 2¼ cups skim milk in large bowl; stir in 3 cups plain flour. Cover; stand in warm place 30 minutes or until foamy. Stir in ⅓ cup olive oil, then 2½ cups plain flour. Knead on floured surface 10 minutes or until smooth and elastic. Place dough in large oiled bowl. Cover; stand in warm place until doubled in size. Meanwhile, drain 1¼ cups halved, pitted black olives on absorbent paper. Turn dough onto floured surface; knead in olives and 2 tablespoons chopped fresh oregano. Roll dough into 12in oval; fold almost in half. Place on large greased oven tray; sift 2 tablespoons of plain flour over dough. Bake in moderately hot oven 45 minutes or until cooked when tested; cool on wire rack.
preparation time 25 minutes (plus standing time)
cooking time 45 minutes (plus cooling time)
serves 10 per serving 8.5g fat; 389 cal

cheese breadsticks

Combine 2oz melted butter, 1 teaspoon dry yeast, 2 tablespoons olive oil, 2 teaspoons sugar, ½ teaspoon salt, 1¼ cups grated parmesan cheese and ¾ cup warm water in large bowl; gradually stir in 2½ cups plain flour. Knead on lightly floured surface 10 minutes or until smooth and elastic. Place dough in large oiled bowl; turn to coat. Stand in warm place 10 minutes. Cut dough into quarters; roll each quarter into 10 logs, about 8in long. Place ¼in apart on lightly greased oven trays. Bake in hot oven 20 minutes or until crisp and browned; cool on wire racks.
preparation time 30 minutes (plus standing time)
cooking time 10 minutes (plus cooling time)
makes 40 per breadstick 3.1g fat; 63 cal

pagnotta

Combine 2 teaspoons dry yeast, ½ teaspoon sugar, 2 teaspoons salt and 3½ cups plain flour in large bowl. Gradually stir in 1¼ cups warm skim milk and 2 teaspoons olive oil until combined. Knead dough on lightly floured surface 2 minutes or until well combined. Place dough in large oiled bowl; turn to coat. Cover; stand in warm place about 30 minutes or until dough doubles in size. Turn dough onto floured surface; knead 10 minutes or until dough is smooth and elastic. Shape dough into 23in log; place on an oiled and floured oven tray. Lightly brush ends with water; gently press together to form a ring. Combine 2 teaspoons olive oil and 2 teaspoons warm water in small bowl; brush over dough. Sift over a little extra flour. Place in cold oven; turn temperature to moderately hot. Bake 40 minutes or until cooked when tested; cool.
preparation time 25 minutes (plus standing time)
cooking time 40 minutes (plus cooling time)
serves 6 per serving 4.2g fat; 350 cal

pasta

For many centuries, the Italian people have embraced pasta with fervor, giving it something of the status of a national dish. The result is a wealth of delicious recipes as varied as the shapes of pasta itself—sometimes rich and hearty, sometimes creamy and delicate, but always easy to prepare and popular with adults and children alike.

rigatoni with eggplant sauce

¼ cup (60ml) olive oil

1 medium onion, chopped finely

2 trimmed sticks celery, chopped finely

1 clove garlic, crushed

2 tablespoons brandy

1 medium eggplant (11oz), sliced thinly

2⅓ cups (580ml) bottled tomato pasta sauce

½ cup tomato paste

½ cup (125ml) water

13oz rigatoni

¼ cup finely grated parmesan cheese

tip before serving, warm large bowls and platters, by placing in a sink of very hot water 10 minutes; dry before using.

1 Heat oil in large saucepan; cook onion, celery and garlic, stirring, until onion softens. Add brandy; cook, stirring, until brandy evaporates. Add eggplant; cook, stirring, until eggplant is tender.

2 Stir in sauce, paste and the water; bring to a boil. Reduce heat; simmer, uncovered, about 10 minutes or until sauce thickens slightly. [Can be made 2 days ahead to this stage and refrigerated, covered.]

3 Meanwhile, cook pasta in large saucepan of boiling water, uncovered, until just tender; drain. Place pasta in large warmed bowl with half of the eggplant sauce; toss gently to combine. Divide pasta among serving plates; top each with remaining sauce. Serve with cheese.

preparation time 10 minutes cooking time 20 minutes serves 4 per serving 16.9g fat; 576 cal

spaghetti marinara

1 tablespoon olive oil

1 medium onion, chopped finely

⅓ cup (80ml) dry white wine

⅓ cup (95g) tomato paste

1lb 14oz canned tomatoes

1lb 11oz seafood marinara mix

¼ cup loosely packed, coarsely chopped
   fresh flat-leaf parsley

13oz spaghetti

tip seafood marinara is a mixture of uncooked, chopped seafood available from fish markets and fishmongers.

1 Heat oil in large frying pan; cook onion, stirring, until soft.

2 Add wine, paste and undrained crushed tomatoes to pan; bring to a boil. Reduce heat; simmer, uncovered, 10 minutes or until sauce thickens slightly.

3 Add marinara mix; cook, stirring occasionally, about 5 minutes or until seafood is cooked through. Stir in parsley.

4 Meanwhile, cook pasta in large saucepan of boiling water, uncovered, until just tender; drain.

5 Serve marinara over pasta.

preparation time 5 minutes cooking time 15 minutes serves 4 per serving 11.6g fat; 671 cal

lasagne

1 tablespoon olive oil

1 medium onion, chopped finely

1 medium carrot, chopped finely

1 trimmed stick celery, chopped finely

2 cloves garlic, crushed

1lb ground beef

⅓ cup (80ml) dry red wine

1lb 14oz canned tomatoes

2 tablespoons tomato paste

½ cup (125ml) water

4 slices prosciutto, chopped finely

1 tablespoon coarsely chopped fresh oregano

2 tablespoons coarsely chopped fresh parsley

18 lasagne sheets

½ cup grated parmesan cheese

cheese sauce

2oz butter

⅓ cup flour

4 cups milk

¾ cup grated parmesan cheese

pinch ground nutmeg

store recipe best made a day ahead; can be made 3 days ahead and refrigerated, covered, or frozen for up to 2 months.

1 Heat oil in large frying pan; cook onion, carrot, celery and garlic, stirring, until onion is soft. Add beef; cook, stirring, until browned. Add wine; bring to a boil. Stir in undrained crushed tomatoes, paste and the water; reduce heat. Simmer, uncovered, about 1 hour or until mixture is thick. Stir in prosciutto and herbs; cool slightly.

2 Place six lasagne sheets into greased shallow 12 cup ovenproof dish. Spread with half of the meat sauce; drizzle with 1 cup of the cheese sauce. Repeat layers again.

3 Top with remaining pasta sheets. Spread with remaining cheese sauce; sprinkle with cheese. Bake in moderate oven about 45 minutes or until pasta is tender and lasagne is browned.

cheese sauce heat butter in large saucepan; cook flour, stirring over heat until flour bubbles and thickens. Remove from heat; gradually stir in milk. Cook, until mixture boils and thickens. Remove from heat; stir in cheese and nutmeg. Cool 10 minutes.

preparation time 40 minutes cooking time 2 hours 10 minutes serves 6 per serving 32.4g fat; 699 cal

cheese and spinach tortellini with gorgonzola sauce

tips ravioli or gnocchi can be substituted for the tortellini.
It's best to choose a ricotta-and-spinach-filled tortellini (or the even simpler ricotta-filled version) when making this sauce, as it doesn't marry overly well with meat-filled pastas.

1oz butter
2 tablespoons plain flour
1 cup (250ml) milk
¾ cup (180ml) cream
4oz gorgonzola cheese, chopped coarsely
1lb 11oz cheese and spinach tortellini
¼ cup loosely packed fresh flat-leaf parsley
freshly ground black pepper

1 Melt butter in medium saucepan; cook flour, stirring, about 2 minutes or until mixture bubbles and thickens.
2 Gradually stir in milk and cream; bring to a boil. Reduce heat; simmer, uncovered, until sauce boils and thickens. Remove from heat; stir in cheese.
3 Meanwhile, cook pasta in large saucepan of boiling water, uncovered, until just tender; drain.
4 Combine pasta with sauce; sprinkle with parsley and pepper.
preparation time 5 minutes cooking time 15 minutes serves 4 per serving 43.8g fat; 718 cal

pappardelle with chili and semi-dried tomato sauce

tip pappardelle is the widest ribbon pasta available; any long pasta such as fettuccine or tagliatelle can be substituted.

2 medium onions, chopped coarsely
2 cloves garlic, quartered
1 cup semi-dried tomatoes in oil, drained
¼ cup tomato paste
2 fresh red Thai chilies, seeded, chopped finely
2 cups (500ml) beef stock

375g pappardelle
¼ cup coarsely chopped fresh flat-leaf parsley
freshly ground black pepper

1 Blend or process onion, garlic, tomatoes, tomato paste and chili until mixture forms a paste.
2 Heat large non-stick frying pan; cook tomato mixture, stirring, 10 minutes. Stir in stock; bring to a boil. Reduce heat; simmer sauce, uncovered, about 10 minutes or until thickened slightly. [Can be made 2 days ahead to this stage and refrigerated, covered, or frozen for up to 6 months.]
3 Meanwhile, cook pasta in large saucepan of boiling water, uncovered, until just tender; drain.
4 Just before serving, gently toss pasta through sauce; sprinkle with parsley and pepper.
preparation time 15 minutes cooking time 25 minutes serves 6 per serving 2.9g fat; 273 cal

spaghetti with herbed ricotta

1lb 2oz spaghetti

1lb fresh ricotta

3 egg yolks

¾ cup (180ml) milk

⅓ cup firmly packed, coarsely chopped fresh flat-leaf parsley

¼ cup firmly packed, coarsely chopped fresh basil

3 green onions, chopped finely

2 cloves garlic, crushed

¼ cup finely grated pepato cheese

freshly ground black pepper

tips pepato can be substituted with another hard cheese, such as romano or an aged provolone.
Feel free to use other herbs, such as chives or oregano, instead of the basil.

1 Cook pasta in large saucepan of boiling water, uncovered, until just tender; drain.

2 Whisk ricotta, yolks and milk in large bowl until smooth; stir in herbs, onion, garlic and cheese.

3 Add pasta to ricotta mixture; toss gently to combine. Sprinkle with pepper to serve.

preparation time 10 minutes cooking time 15 minutes serves 4 per serving 21.7g fat; 682 cal

fettuccine carbonara

4 bacon slices, chopped coarsely

13oz fettuccine

3 egg yolks, beaten

1 cup (250ml) cream

½ cup finely grated parmesan cheese

2 tablespoons coarsely chopped fresh chives

tip   pancetta or prosciutto can be substituted for the bacon, and grated romano or pepato can be substituted for the parmesan.

1   Cook bacon in small heated frying pan, stirring, until crisp; drain.

2   Just before serving, cook pasta in large saucepan of boiling water, uncovered, until just tender; drain.

3   Combine pasta in warmed large bowl with yolks, cream and cheese; sprinkle with chives and freshly ground black pepper, if desired.

preparation time 10 minutes   cooking time 10 minutes   serves 4   per serving   42g fat; 767 cal

fettuccine with meatballs in rosemary paprika sauce

9oz lean ground beef

½ cup stale breadcrumbs

1 tablespoon finely chopped fresh parsley

1 tablespoon finely chopped fresh chives

1 egg white

1 teaspoon worcestershire sauce

2 teaspoons olive oil

9oz fettuccine

rosemary paprika sauce

15oz canned tomatoes

1 cup (250ml) water

2 tablespoons dry red wine

1 medium onion, chopped finely

½ teaspoon Worcestershire sauce

1 teaspoon sweet paprika

3 sprigs rosemary

1   Combine beef, breadcrumbs, parsley, chives, egg white and sauce in large bowl. Shape mixture into small meatballs.

2   Heat oil in medium non-stick saucepan; cook meatballs until well browned all over and cooked through. Drain on absorbent paper.

3   Meanwhile, cook pasta in large saucepan of boiling water until tender; drain.

4   Add meatballs to rosemary paprika sauce; mix well. Stir until heated through. [Can be made 2 days ahead to this stage and refrigerated, covered, or frozen for up to 3 months.]

5   Serve pasta with meatballs in rosemary paprika sauce.

rosemary paprika sauce   combine undrained crushed tomatoes with remaining ingredients in medium saucepan; bring to a boil. Reduce heat; simmer, uncovered, about 20 minutes or until thickened slightly.

preparation time 15 minutes   cooking time 45 minutes   serves 2   per serving   15.8g fat; 786 cal

chicken and prosciutto cannelloni

2oz butter

¼ cup flour

⅔ cup (160ml) milk

1½ cups (375ml) chicken stock

½ cup finely grated parmesan cheese

14oz fontina cheese, grated coarsely

1 tablespoon olive oil

2 medium onions, chopped finely

3 cloves garlic, crushed

2lbs 4oz ground chicken

2 tablespoons finely chopped fresh sage

1lb 14oz canned tomatoes

½ cup (125ml) dry white wine

¼ cup (70g) tomato paste

3 teaspoons sugar

12 fresh lasagne sheets

24 slices prosciutto (13oz)

tip pancetta or double-smoked ham can be substituted for the prosciutto.

1 Heat butter in medium saucepan; cook flour, stirring, until flour thickens and bubbles. Gradually stir in milk and stock; cook, stirring, until sauce boils and thickens. Remove from heat; stir in parmesan and a quarter of the fontina.

2 Heat oil in large saucepan; cook onion and garlic, stirring, until onion is soft. Add chicken; cook, stirring, until browned. Stir in sage. Combine chicken and cheese sauce in large bowl; cool.

3 Combine undrained crushed tomatoes, wine, paste and sugar in same large pan; cook, stirring, 10 minutes. Cool 10 minutes; blend or process, in batches, until smooth.

4 Cut pasta sheets and prosciutto slices in half crossways. Place two pieces of prosciutto on each piece of pasta. Top each with ¼ cup chicken mixture; roll to enclose filling. Repeat with remaining pasta, prosciutto and chicken mixture.

5 Oil two 12-cup ovenproof dishes. Pour a quarter of the tomato sauce into base of each prepared dish; place half of the pasta rolls, seam-side down, in each dish. Pour remaining tomato sauce over rolls; sprinkle each dish with remaining fontina. [Can be made 2 days ahead to this stage and refrigerated, covered, or frozen for up to 2 months.]

6 Bake cannelloni, covered, at 350º F for 30 minutes. Uncover, bake further 15 minutes or until cheese melts and browns. Serve with a green salad, if desired.

preparation time 30 minutes cooking time 1 hour 10 minutes serves 8 per serving 40.3g fat; 714 cal

bow ties and salmon in lemon cream

13oz bow ties pasta
1 medium lemon
15oz canned red salmon, drained, flaked
½ cup (125ml) cream
4 green onions, sliced thinly

1 Cook pasta in large saucepan of boiling water, uncovered, until just tender; drain.
2 Meanwhile, using zester, remove rind from lemon. Place rind and pasta in large saucepan with salmon, cream and onion; stir over low heat until hot.
preparation time 10 minutes   cooking time 15 minutes serves 4 per serving 24.7g fat; 601 cal

pasta primavera

13oz small spiral pasta
1 tablespoon olive oil
1 medium onion, chopped finely
3 cloves garlic, crushed
11oz yellow patty-pan squash, quartered
1 medium red pepper, sliced thinly

7oz sugar snap peas
1 medium carrot, cut into ribbons
1¼ cups (310ml) cream
1 tablespoon seeded mustard
2 tablespoons finely chopped fresh
   flat-leaf parsley

1 Cook pasta in large saucepan of boiling water, uncovered, until just tender; drain.
2 Meanwhile, heat oil in large saucepan; cook onion and garlic, stirring, until onion softens. Add squash; cook, stirring, until just tender. Add pepper, peas and carrot; cook, stirring, until pepper is just tender.
3 Place pasta in pan with vegetables; add combined remaining ingredients. Stir over low heat until just hot.
preparation time 15 minutes   cooking time 15 minutes serves 4 per serving 38.9g fat; 722 cal

spaghetti puttanesca

¼ cup (60ml) olive oil

2 cloves garlic, crushed

4 medium tomatoes (1lb 11oz), chopped coarsely

½ cup finely chopped fresh parsley

12 stuffed olives, sliced thinly

2oz canned anchovy fillets, chopped finely

1 tablespoon finely chopped fresh basil

pinch chili powder

13oz spaghetti

1 Heat oil in medium saucepan; cook garlic until just changed in color.

2 Add tomato, parsley, olives, anchovy, basil and chili powder; cook further 3 minutes.

3 Meanwhile, cook pasta in large saucepan of boiling water, uncovered, until just tender; drain.

4 Combine pasta in large warmed bowl, with sauce; toss gently.

preparation time 15 minutes cooking time 20 minutes serves 4 per serving 16.9g fat; 489 cal

spaghetti with pesto

2 cups coarsely chopped fresh basil
2 tablespoons pine nuts, toasted
2 cloves garlic
⅓ cup (80ml) olive oil
¼ cup finely grated parmesan cheese
13oz spaghetti

store pesto can be made 2 weeks ahead and refrigerated in sterilised jar with a thin layer of olive oil over top, or frozen, in freezer container, for up to 3 months.

1 Blend or process basil, pine nuts and garlic until smooth. With processor operating, add oil in thin stream; process further 1 second.
2 Place basil mixture in medium bowl. Add cheese; mix until combined.
3 Cook pasta in large saucepan of boiling water, uncovered, until just tender; drain.
4 Combine pasta with pesto in large warmed bowl; toss gently.

preparation time 15 minutes   cooking time 15 minutes serves 4 per serving 26.5 fat; 563 cal

ricotta and swiss chard lasagne

2lb 4oz Swiss chard, trimmed
3 eggs, beaten lightly
2 cups ricotta cheese
¼ cup coarsely grated parmesan cheese

3 green onions, chopped finely
1½ cups (375ml) bottled tomato pasta sauce
12 sheets instant lasagne
1 cup coarsely grated cheddar cheese

1 Boil, steam or microwave Swiss chard until just wilted; drain. Squeeze as much liquid as possible from Swiss chard; chop coarsely. Combine egg, ricotta, parmesan and onion in large bowl; stir in Swiss chard.
2 Spread half of the pasta sauce over base of oiled shallow baking dish. Cover with three sheets lasagne; top with a third of the Swiss chard mixture. Cover Swiss chard layer with three sheets of the lasagne; repeat layering with remaining Swiss chard mixture and remaining lasagne sheets. Top lasagne with remaining pasta sauce; sprinkle with cheddar.
3 Cover lasagne with foil; bake at 350º F for 40 minutes. [Can be made 2 days ahead to this stage and refrigerated, covered, or frozen for up to 3 months.]
4 Remove foil; bake 20 minutes or until browned on top.

preparation time 15 minutes cooking time 1 hour 5 minutes serves 4 per serving 28.4g fat; 570 cal

fettuccine boscaiola

2 teaspoons olive oil
7oz button mushrooms, sliced thickly
2 cloves garlic, crushed
7oz shaved ham, chopped coarsely
¼ cup (60ml) dry white wine
1¼ cups (310ml) cream
1lb 2oz fettuccine
2 tablespoons coarsely chopped fresh chives

1 Heat oil in large saucepan; cook mushrooms, garlic and ham, stirring, until ingredients are browned lightly. Add wine; boil, uncovered, until wine reduces by half.
2 Add cream to mushroom mixture; reduce heat. Simmer, uncovered, until sauce thickens slightly.
3 Meanwhile, cook pasta in large saucepan of boiling water, uncovered, until just tender; drain.
4 Add chives and pasta to sauce; toss gently until mixed well.
preparation time 10 minutes cooking time 20 minutes serves 4 per serving 32.6g fat; 784 cal

chicken ravioli with tarragon sauce

1lb 11oz ground chicken
2 green onions, sliced thinly
2 teaspoons finely grated lemon rind
56 gow gee wrappers
1 egg, beaten lightly
2 teaspoons olive oil

1 medium onion, chopped finely
2 cloves garlic, crushed
½ cup (125ml) dry white wine
1 tablespoon dijon mustard
2⅓ cups (580ml) cream
2 tablespoons shredded fresh tarragon leaves

1 Combine chicken, green onion and rind in medium bowl.
2 Brush one wrapper at a time with egg. Place a rounded teaspoon of the chicken mixture in center of wrapper. Fold over to enclose filling; press edge to seal. Repeat with remaining wrappers, egg and chicken mixture. Place ravioli, in single layer, on tray. Cover; refrigerate 30 minutes. [Can be made ahead to this stage and frozen for up to 2 months.]
3 Heat oil in medium saucepan; cook brown onion and garlic, stirring, until onion is just browned. Add wine; cook, stirring, about 5 minutes or until wine reduces by a half. Stir in mustard and cream; cook sauce, stirring, until mixture just boils.
4 Meanwhile, cook ravioli, uncovered, in large saucepan of boiling water until each ravioli floats to the top. Remove ravioli with slotted spoon; drain. Return ravioli to pan; add tarragon and cream sauce. Toss gently until warmed through.
preparation time 25 minutes (plus refrigeration time) cooking time 30 minutes serves 8
per serving 38.5g fat; 532 cal

fettuccine alfredo

13oz fettuccine
3oz butter, chopped coarsely
⅔ cup (150ml) cream
1 cup finely grated parmesan cheese
2 tablespoons finely chopped fresh flat-leaf parsley

1 Cook pasta in large saucepan of boiling water, uncovered, until just tender; drain. Keep pasta warm while preparing sauce.
2 Place butter and cream in medium saucepan. Stir over low heat until butter melts and combines well with cream; remove from heat. Add cheese; stir until sauce is blended and smooth.
3 Spoon sauce over hot pasta; toss well. Serve sprinkled with parsley.
preparation time 5 minutes cooking time 15 minutes serves 4 per serving 42.3g fat; 714 cal

spaghetti bolognese

2 tablespoons olive oil

1 large brown onion, chopped finely

1lb 11oz ground beef

425g canned tomatoes

1 teaspoon fresh basil

1 teaspoon fresh oregano

½ teaspoon fresh thyme

⅓ cup tomato paste

4 cups water

9oz spaghetti

grated parmesan cheese

tip a true bolognese sauce contains no garlic, however two crushed cloves of garlic can be added to the tomatoes in step 2, if desired.

1 Heat oil in large saucepan; cook onion until golden brown. Add beef to pan; cook until beef browns, mashing with fork occasionally to break up lumps. Pour off any surplus fat.

2 Push undrained tomatoes through sieve; add to pan. Add herbs, paste and the water; bring to a boil. Reduce heat; simmer, very gently, uncovered, about 1½ hours, or until nearly all liquid evaporates. [Can be made 2 days ahead to this stage and refrigerated, covered, or frozen for up to 3 months.]

3 Cook spaghetti in large saucepan of boiling water until just tender; drain well.

4 Arrange hot spaghetti in individual serving bowls; top with sauce. Sprinkle with cheese.

preparation time 15 minutes cooking time 2 hours 15 minutes serves 4 per serving 28.7g fat; 445 cal

pagli e fieno

2 teaspoons olive oil

5 green onions, sliced thinly

2 cloves garlic, crushed

1lb 2oz button mushrooms, sliced thickly

1 tablespoon dry white wine

1¼ cups (310ml) cream

¼ cup coarsely chopped fresh flat-leaf parsley

5oz plain fettuccine

5oz spinach-flavored fettuccine

1 Heat oil in medium saucepan; cook onion and garlic, stirring, until onion softens.

2 Add mushrooms; cook, stirring, until just browned. Add wine and cream; bring to a boil. Reduce heat; simmer, uncovered, about 5 minutes or until sauce thickens slightly. Stir in parsley.

3 Meanwhile, cook both pastas in large saucepan of boiling water, uncovered, until just tender; drain. Place pasta in large warmed bowl with sauce; toss gently to combine.

preparation time 10 minutes cooking time 15 minutes serves 4 per serving 36g fat; 557 cal

penne arrabiata

1 tablespoon olive oil

2 medium brown onions, chopped finely

5 cloves garlic, crushed

3 fresh red Thai chilies, chopped finely

2⅓ cups (580ml) bottled tomato pasta sauce

2 teaspoons balsamic vinegar

13oz penne

¼ cup finely grated parmesan cheese

tip leftover pasta and sauce can be placed in an oiled ovenproof dish, covered with mozzarella and baked in moderate oven until heated through and cheese bubbles.

1 Heat oil in large saucepan; cook onion, garlic and chili, stirring, until onion softens. Add sauce and vinegar; bring to a boil. Reduce heat; simmer, uncovered, about 5 minutes or until sauce thickens slightly. [Can be made a day ahead to this stage and refrigerated, covered, or frozen for up to 6 months.]

2 Meanwhile, cook pasta in large saucepan of boiling water, uncovered, until just tender; drain. Combine pasta with sauce; sprinkle with cheese.

preparation time 10 minutes cooking time 15 minutes serves 4 per serving 7.6g fat; 453 cal

spaghetti napoletana

2 teaspoons olive oil

1 small onion, chopped finely

3 cloves garlic, crushed

1lb 14oz canned tomatoes

¼ cup coarsely chopped, firmly packed fresh basil

⅓ cup coarsely chopped, firmly packed fresh flat-leaf parsley

13oz spaghetti

tip if you cook this sauce even longer, until it reduces by half, it makes a good pizza-base sauce or, with capers stirred through it, a delicious topping for chicken or veal scaloppine.

1 Heat oil in large saucepan; cook onion and garlic, stirring, until onion softens.

2 Add undrained crushed tomatoes; bring to a boil. Reduce heat; simmer, uncovered, about 20 minutes or until reduced by about a third. Stir in basil and parsley. [Can be made a day ahead to this stage and refrigerated, covered, or frozen for up to 3 months.]

3 Meanwhile, cook pasta in large saucepan of boiling water, uncovered, until just tender; drain. Serve pasta topped with sauce.

preparation time 5 minutes   cooking time 25 minutes serves 4 per serving 4g fat; 397 cal

bruschetta

creamy mushroom

Cut ½ loaf ciabatta into thick slices. Toast under hot grill until browned lightly; while still hot, rub one side of each toast with halved garlic cloves. Place toast in single layer on tray; drizzle evenly with ¼ cup olive oil. Heat ¼ cup olive oil in medium frying pan, add 1 clove crushed garlic and 9oz finely chopped flat mushrooms; cook, stirring, over heat until very soft. Add 1 tablespoon lemon juice; stir over high heat until absorbed. Pour in ½ cup cream; stir to combine. Gently stir in 4oz thinly sliced button mushrooms; stir over high heat until almost all liquid is absorbed. Remove from heat; stir in 2 tablespoons finely grated parmesan cheese. Top bruschetta with mushroom mixture; sprinkle with ¼ cup coarsely chopped fresh chives. Serve.

preparation time 20 minutes cooking time 15 minutes serves 8 per serving 22.7g fat; 291 cal

olive, anchovy and caper

Cut ½ loaf ciabatta into thick slices. Toast under hot grill until browned lightly; while still hot, rub one side of each toast with halved garlic cloves. Place toast in single layer on tray; drizzle evenly with ¼ cup olive oil. Combine 3 drained, finely chopped anchovy fillets, ½ cup seeded finely chopped black olives, 1 tablespoon drained baby capers, 1 tablespoon lemon juice and 1 tablespoon olive oil in small bowl. Just before serving, divide olive mixture among bruschetta; top with ⅓ cup parmesan cheese flakes, then 2 tablespoons marjoram.

preparation time 15 minutes cooking time 5 minutes serves 8 per serving 11.3g fat; 189 cal

tomato and rocket

Cut ½ loaf ciabatta into thick slices. Toast under hot grill until browned lightly; while still hot, rub one side of each toast with halved garlic cloves. Place toast in single layer on tray; drizzle evenly with ¼ cup olive oil. Combine 3 medium finely chopped egg tomatoes and ½ small finely chopped red onion in small bowl. Just before serving, top bruschetta with tomato mixture, then 1oz baby rocket leaves.

preparation time 15 minutes cooking time 5 minutes serves 8 per serving 7.8g fat; 150 cal

roasted pepper and prosciutto

Cut ½ loaf ciabatta into thick slices. Toast under hot grill until browned lightly; while still hot, rub one side of each toast with halved garlic cloves. Place toast in single layer on tray; drizzle evenly with ¼ cup olive oil. Quarter 2 medium red peppers; remove and discard seeds and membranes. Place pepper on oven tray; roast under hot grill or in very hot oven, skin-side up, until skin blisters and blackens. Cover pepper pieces in plastic 5 minutes. Peel away skin; discard. Cut pepper into thin strips. Cook 5 coarsely chopped slices prosciutto in medium heated frying pan until crisp. Add pepper and 1 tablespoon balsamic vinegar to pan; stir to combine. Cool to room temperature. Just before serving divide mixture among bruschetta; top with 2 tablespoons fresh oregano.

preparation time 20 minutes cooking time 7 minutes serves 8 per serving 8.4g fat; 165 cal

pizza

If you've only eaten the fast food variety, you haven't really tried pizza. Despite coming a long way from its cheese and tomato origins, the basic principle is the same—fresh, yeasty dough topped with a range of ingredients. Purchased bases are certainly convenient, but our easy homemade ones will convert you!

marinara pizza

9oz medium uncooked shrimp
9oz marinara seafood mix
1 tablespoon olive oil
1 medium white onion, chopped finely
1 clove garlic, crushed
15oz canned tomatoes

⅓ cup (80ml) dry white wine
12in homemade or purchased pizza base
3 cloves garlic, crushed, extra
¼ cup tomato paste
2 teaspoons dried oregano

tip if you prefer to use just shrimp for this pizza, you will need 18oz medium uncooked shrimp.

1 Peel and devein shrimp. Rinse marinara mix under cold running water; drain well.

2 Heat oil in large frying pan; cook onion and garlic, stirring, until onion is soft. Add undrained crushed tomatoes and wine. Simmer, uncovered, until sauce thickens.

3 Add seafood; simmer, uncovered, 2 minutes or until seafood just changes colour. Remove seafood with slotted spoon. Continue simmering sauce until very thick.

4 Place pizza base on oiled pizza tray. Spread with combined garlic, paste and oregano. Spoon seafood, then sauce over pizza.

5 Bake, uncovered, at 400º F for about 20 minutes or until base is cooked though and seafood is tender.

preparation time 25 minutes cooking time 40 minutes serves 4 per serving 9.5g fat: 381 cal

tomato and onion pita pizzas

4 wholemeal pita
¼ cup (60ml) bottled tomato pasta sauce
1 cup grated cheddar cheese
2 medium tomatoes sliced thinly
1 medium onion, sliced thinly
¼ cup pitted black olives, halved

1 Place pita in single layer on lightly oiled oven tray. Spread each pita with pasta sauce; top with half of the cheese. Top with tomato, onion and olives; sprinkle with remaining cheese.

2 Bake pizzas at 425º F for 15 minutes or until browned lightly.

preparation time 15 minutes cooking time 15 minutes serves 4 per serving 16.7g fat; 389 cal

napoletana pizza

11oz mozzarella, sliced thinly
¼ cup coarsely torn basil
basic pizza dough
2 teaspoons instant yeast
½ teaspoon salt
2½ cups flour
1 cup (250ml) warm water
1 tablespoon olive oil

basic tomato pizza sauce
1 tablespoon olive oil
1 small white onion, chopped finely
2 cloves garlic, crushed
15oz canned tomatoes
¼ cup tomato paste
1 teaspoon sugar
1 tablespoon fresh oregano

tip purchased pizza bases can be used in place of the basic pizza dough.

store basic pizza dough can be made 3 hours ahead and refrigerated, covered. Remove from refrigerator 10 minutes before using.

1 Halve basic pizza dough; roll out each half on lightly floured surface to form 12in round. Place on two oiled pizza trays. Spread each with half of the basic tomato pizza sauce; top with cheese.
2 Bake, uncovered, at 400° F for about 15 minutes or until crust is golden and cheese is bubbling. Sprinkle each with basil before serving.

basic pizza dough combine yeast, salt and sifted flour in large bowl; mix well. Gradually stir in the water and oil. Knead on well floured surface about 10 minutes or until smooth and elastic. Place dough in large oiled bowl; stand in warm place about 30 minutes or until dough doubles in size. Knead dough on lightly floured surface until smooth. Roll out dough as required or to fit pizza tray.

basic tomato pizza sauce heat oil in medium frying pan; cook onion, stirring occasionally, over low heat until soft and transparent. Stir in garlic, undrained, crushed tomatoes, paste, sugar and oregano. Simmer, uncovered, about 15 minutes or until mixture thickens. [Can be made 2 days ahead and refrigerated, covered, or frozen for up to 6 months.]

preparation time 20 minutes (plus standing time) cooking time 30 minutes serves 6
per serving 18.1g fat; 450 cal

roast garlic and potato pizza

5 medium potatoes (2lbs 4oz), halved

4 cloves garlic, crushed

¼ cup fresh oregano

1 large onion, sliced thickly

¼ cup (60ml) olive oil

7 small tomatoes (2lbs), halved

2 teaspoons sugar

12in round homemade or purchased
  pizza base

1½ cups coarsely grated
  mozzarella cheese

¼ cup finely shredded fresh basil

1 Boil, steam or microwave potato until just tender, drain. Cut each potato half in half again; place in large shallow baking dish with garlic, oregano and onion. Drizzle with 2 tablespoons of the oil. Bake, uncovered, at 475° F for about 20 minutes or until onion is soft and potato is browned lightly.

2 Meanwhile, combine tomato and remaining oil in medium baking dish; bake, uncovered, at 475° F for about 30 minutes or until tomato is browned and soft. Blend or process tomato with sugar until just chopped coarsely. [Can be made a day ahead to this stage and refrigerated, covered.]

3 Spread tomato mixture on pizza base; top with 1 cup of the cheese, then potato mixture. Sprinkle remaining cheese and basil over the top; bake, uncovered, at 425° F, for about 30 minutes or until cheese is browned and pizza base is crisp.

preparation time 25 minutes ooking time 1 hour 10 minutes serves 4 per serving 25g fat; 637 cal

pepperoni in a flash

12in homemade or purchased pizza base

⅓ cup tomato paste

2 teaspoons dried oregano

2 cups grated mozzarella cheese

¼ cup grated parmesan cheese

5oz sliced pepperoni

½ cup pitted black olives

tip any salami, cabanossi or ham can be substituted for the pepperoni.

1 Place pizza base on oiled pizza tray. Spread base with combined tomato paste and oregano; sprinkle with two-thirds of the combined cheeses. Top with pepperoni and olives, then remaining cheeses.

2 Bake, uncovered, at 400° F, for about 20 minutes or until base is cooked through and cheese is bubbling.

preparation time 10 minutes   cooking time 20 minutes serves 4 per serving 29g fat; 550 cal

vegetarian calzone

2 teaspoons dry yeast

1 teaspoon sugar

1½ cups (375ml) warm water

4 cups flour

1 teaspoon salt

½ teaspoon cracked black pepper

2 tablespoons olive oil

1 cup coarsely grated cheddar cheese

vegetable filling

1 small eggplant (8oz), chopped coarsely

coarse cooking salt

1 tablespoon olive oil

1 large onion (7oz), chopped coarsely

2 cloves garlic, crushed

1 medium red pepper, chopped coarsely

2 medium zucchini, chopped coarsely

2 trimmed sticks celery, chopped coarsely

2 tablespoons tomato paste

½ cup (125ml) vegetable stock

1 Whisk yeast, sugar and the water together in small bowl. Cover; stand in warm place about 10 minutes or until mixture is frothy.

2 Place flour, salt and pepper in large bowl. Stir in yeast mixture and oil; mix to a firm dough. Turn dough onto floured surface; knead about 10 minutes or until smooth and elastic. Place dough in large oiled bowl. Cover; stand in warm place about 30 minutes or until doubled in size.

3 Transfer dough to floured surface; knead until smooth. Divide dough into four pieces; roll each piece to a 9½in round. Spread one half of each round with a quarter of the vegetable filling; top with a quarter of the cheese. Fold plain dough over cheese to enclose filling; press edges together.

4 Place calzone on oiled oven trays; brush with a little extra oil. Cut two small slits on top of each calzone; bake, uncovered, in hot oven about 20 minutes or until browned.

vegetable filling place eggplant in strainer. Sprinkle with salt; stand 30 minutes. Rinse eggplant under cold running water; drain on absorbent paper. Heat oil in large frying pan; cook onion and garlic, stirring, until onion is soft. Add eggplant, pepper, zucchini and celery; cook, stirring, about 5 minutes or until vegetables are soft. Add paste and stock. Cook, stirring, until mixture thickens; cool. [Can be made a day ahead to this stage and refrigerated, covered, or frozen for up to 2 months.]

preparation time 40 minutes (plus standing time) cooking time 50 minutes serves 4
per serving 26.8g fat; 833 cal

pizza with prosciutto and ricotta

3 medium tomatoes (8oz)

3 x 10in homemade or purchased pizza bases

½ cup tomato paste

11oz baby spinach

1 large red onion (11oz), sliced thinly

9 slices prosciutto, halved

¼ cup loosely packed, coarsely chopped
  fresh basil

1½ cups ricotta cheese

¼ cup pine nuts

¼ cup (60ml) olive oil

2 cloves garlic, crushed

1 Cut each tomato into eight wedges.
2 Place pizza bases on oven trays. Spread each base with a third of the tomato paste; top with equal amounts of tomato, spinach, onion, prosciutto, basil, cheese and pine nuts. Drizzle each pizza with equal amounts of combined oil and garlic.
3 Bake, uncovered, at 475° F for about 15 minutes or until pizza tops are browned lightly and bases are crisp.
preparation time 15 minutes cooking time 15 minutes serves 6 per serving 27.6g fat; 699 cal

salami, mushroom and oregano pizza

tips split a purchased base in half for a thin crust pizza. Use cut-side up and bake about 5 minutes less than the time stated.
Use your choice of mild or hot salami for this pizza.

12in homemade or purchased pizza base

¼ cup tomato paste

2 teaspoons dried oregano

⅓ cup (80ml) bottled tomato pasta sauce

½ cup (5oz) chopped cooked Swiss chard

2oz button mushrooms, sliced thinly

4oz sliced salami

¾ cup grated mozzarella cheese

1 Place pizza base on lightly oiled pizza tray. Spread combined tomato paste and oregano over pizza base. Top with pasta sauce, Swiss chard, mushrooms, then salami. Sprinkle with cheese.
2 Bake, uncovered, at 425° F, for about 20 minutes or until base is cooked through and cheese is bubbling.
preparation time 15 minutes cooking time 20 minutes serves 4 per serving 16.5g fat; 380 cal

roasted tomato, goat cheese and chicken pizza

1lb 2oz cherry tomatoes, halved
2 tablespoons balsamic vinegar
2 tablespoons brown sugar
2 chicken breast fillets (12oz)
12in round homemade or purchased pizza base
2 tablespoons coarsely chopped fresh coriander
3oz goat cheese
1oz rocket

tips lebanese bread can be substituted for prepared pizza base. Use baking paper to prevent the skin of the tomatoes sticking to oven tray.

1 Place tomatoes on oven tray lined with baking paper; drizzle with combined vinegar and sugar. Bake, uncovered, at 475° F for about 25 minutes or until tomatoes are soft.
2 Meanwhile, cook chicken on heated oiled grill plate (or grill or barbecue) until browned both sides and cooked through. Cool 5 minutes; cut into thin slices. Place pizza base on oven tray; bake, uncovered, at 425° F for about 10 minutes or until browned lightly.
3 Top pizza with tomato, chicken, coriander and crumbled cheese. Bake, uncovered, at 475° F for 10 minutes or until pizza is browned and crisp.
4 Just before serving, top with rocket.
preparation time 25 minutes cooking time 35 minutes serves 2 per serving 17.6g fat; 780 cal

pesto, bocconcini and artichoke pizza

12in homemade or purchased pizza base
7oz jar pesto
4oz marinated eggplant slices
7oz char-grilled pepper slices

2 drained marinated artichoke hearts,
    sliced thickly
6 bocconcini, sliced thickly
2 tablespoons pine nuts

tip the same amount of ingredients used to top a 12in pizza will top four mini pizza bases.

1 Place pizza base on oiled pizza tray. Spread pesto over base; top with eggplant, pepper and artichokes. Arrange bocconcini on top; sprinkle with pine nuts.
2 Bake, uncovered, at 400º F for about 20 minutes or until base is cooked through and cheese is bubbling.

preparation time 10 minutes cooking time 25 minutes serves 4 per serving 40.1g fat; 615 cal

spinach, anchovy and olive pizza

12in homemade or purchased pizza base
⅓ cup (80ml) bottled tomato pasta sauce
½ cup coarsely chopped cooked spinach
½ cup grated mozzarella cheese
⅓ cup grated parmesan cheese
¼ cup grated cheddar cheese
½ cup black olives
6 anchovy fillets, drained

tip use frozen spinach, which has been cooked and cooled, for this recipe.

1 Place pizza base on lightly oiled pizza tray; spread with pasta sauce.
2 Squeeze as much liquid as possible from spinach. Spread spinach over pasta sauce; top with combined cheeses. Sprinkle olives and anchovies over top.
3 Bake, uncovered, at 400º F for about 20 minutes or until base is cooked through and cheese is bubbling.

preparation time 15 minutes cooking time 35 minutes serves 4 per serving 10.7g fat; 321 cal

swiss chard and feta pizza

2 teaspoons dry yeast

1 teaspoon sugar

2½ cups flour

1 cup (250ml) warm water

½ teaspoon salt

2 tablespoons olive oil

¼ cup semolina

1lb 2oz Swiss chard

1 cup crumbled feta cheese

⅓ cup finely grated parmesan cheese

10 cherry tomatoes (4oz), halved

tomato sauce

1 tablespoon olive oil

1 medium onion,
   chopped coarsely

2 cloves garlic, crushed

15oz canned tomatoes

½ cup tomato paste

¼ cup coarsely chopped fresh basil

1 teaspoon sugar

1 Combine yeast, sugar, 1 tablespoon of the flour and the water in small bowl; whisk until yeast dissolves. Cover; stand in warm place about 10 minutes or until mixture is frothy.

2 Combine remaining sifted flour and salt in processor; pour in combined yeast mixture and oil while motor is operating. Process until dough forms a ball. Turn dough onto floured surface; knead 10 minutes or until dough is smooth and elastic. Place dough in oiled large bowl. Cover; stand in warm place about 30 minutes or until dough doubles in size.

3 Turn dough onto surface sprinkled with half of the semolina; knead 1 minute. Place dough on oiled large oven tray sprinkled with remaining semolina; press dough into a 12½in square.

4 Boil, steam or microwave Swiss chard until wilted. Drain; cool. Squeeze as much liquid as possible from Swiss chard; chop Swiss chard finely. Spread pizza base with tomato sauce. Spread evenly with Swiss chard, cheeses and tomato. Bake at 475º F for about 20 minutes.

tomato sauce heat oil in medium saucepan; cook onion and garlic, stirring, until onion is soft. Stir in undrained crushed tomatoes, paste, basil and sugar; simmer, uncovered, about 5 minutes or until thickened.

preparation time 25 minutes (plus standing time) cooking time 30 minutes serves 6
per serving 19.5g fat; 481 cal

rice, gnocchi & polenta

While pasta might be popularly known as the national dish, there are also areas of Italy—principally in the rice- and corn-growing north—where rice, gnocchi and polenta enjoy a similar esteem. Here, creamy risotto, melt-in-the mouth gnocchi and golden polenta feature in a selection of delicious alternatives to pasta.

gnocchi al quattro formaggi

¼ cup (60ml) dry white wine

1 cup mascarpone cheese

1 cup coarsely grated fontina cheese

½ cup coarsely grated parmesan cheese

¼ cup (60ml) milk

1lb 6oz gnocchi

3oz gorgonzola cheese, crumbled

freshly ground black pepper

1 Bring wine to a boil in large saucepan. Boil, uncovered, until wine reduces by half; reduce heat. Add mascarpone; stir until mixture is smooth. Add fontina, parmesan and milk; cook, stirring, until cheeses melt and sauce is smooth.

2 Meanwhile, cook gnocchi, uncovered, in large saucepan of boiling water, until gnocchi rise to the surface. Remove with a slotted spoon; drain.

3 Add gnocchi and gorgonzola to sauce; toss gently to combine. Sprinkle with pepper.

preparation time 10 minutes   cooking time 10 minutes serves 4 per serving 52.3g fat; 730 cal

risotto cakes with basil sauce and pancetta

½ cup (125ml) dry white wine

1 medium onion, chopped finely

1 clove garlic, crushed

1 cup arborio rice

3 cups (750ml) chicken stock

2 tablespoons finely chopped fresh parsley

2 tablespoons finely chopped fresh chives

2 tablespoons finely grated parmesan cheese

1 egg white, beaten lightly

4 slices pancetta (2oz)

4 oak leaf lettuce leaves

basil sauce

1 teaspoon cornflour

1 teaspoon water

¾ cup (180ml) low-fat evaporated milk

1 tablespoon coarsely chopped fresh basil

1 Heat 2 tablespoons of the wine in large saucepan; cook onion and garlic, stirring, about 2 minutes or until onion softens.

2 Add rice and remaining wine; cook, stirring, about 3 minutes or until wine reduces by half. Stir in stock; bring to a boil. Reduce heat; simmer, covered, 15 minutes, stirring halfway through cooking. Remove from heat; stir in parsley, chives and cheese. Cool; stir in egg white. Using hands, shape risotto mixture into four patties. [Can be made a day ahead to this stage and refrigerated, covered.]

3 Place pancetta on oven tray. Bake, uncovered, at 425º F for about 5 minutes or until crisp; drain on absorbent paper. Break pancetta into pieces.

4 Cook risotto cakes in large heated lightly oiled frying pan until browned both sides. Place cakes on oven tray; bake, uncovered, at 350º F for about 10 minutes or until hot.

5 Serve risotto cakes on lettuce leaves. Drizzle with basil sauce; top with pancetta.

basil sauce blend cornflour with the water in small saucepan; add milk. Stir over heat until mixture boils and thickens slightly; stir in basil.

preparation time 20 minutes cooking time 45 minutes serves 4 per serving 3.6g fat; 293 cal

pumpkin gnocchi with rocket pesto

1lb 13oz coarsely chopped pumpkin
1 tablespoon olive oil
2 large potatoes (1lb 5oz), chopped coarsely
1 egg, beaten lightly
1 egg yolk
2 cups flour
2⅓ cups (580ml) cream

rocket pesto
1 cup firmly packed baby rocket
½ cup shelled pistachios, toasted
2 cloves garlic, quartered
½ cup coarsely grated parmesan cheese
¼ cup (60ml) olive oil

1 Toss pumpkin with oil in large baking dish. Bake, uncovered, at 425º F for about 45 minutes or until pumpkin is tender. Boil, steam or microwave potato until tender; drain.
2 Mash pumpkin and potato in large bowl until smooth; stir in egg and yolk. Using floured hand, mix in flour. Turn pumpkin mixture onto floured surface; knead about 2 minutes or until smooth.
3 Using floured hands, roll heaped teaspoons of pumpkin mixture into gnocchi-shaped ovals. Place each oval in palm of hand; press with inverted floured fork tines to flatten gnocchi slightly and make grooved imprint. [Can be made a day ahead to this stage and refrigerated, covered, or frozen for up to 3 months.]
4 Cook gnocchi, in batches, in large saucepan of boiling water; cook, uncovered, about 3 minutes or until gnocchi float to the surface. Remove from pan with slotted spoon; drain.
5 Working quickly, while gnocchi are cooking, heat cream with 2 tablespoons of the rocket pesto in medium saucepan. Serve gnocchi with cream sauce; top with additional rocket pesto to taste.
rocket pesto blend or process rocket, nuts, garlic and cheese until chopped coarsely. With motor operating, gradually pour in oil; process until mixture forms a thick paste. [Can be made a day ahead and refrigerated, covered, or frozen for up to 2 months.]
preparation time 25 minutes cooking time 25 minutes serves 8 per serving 51.3g fat; 701 cal

lemon risotto

4 cups chicken stock

1 cup (250ml) dry white wine

2 teaspoons finely grated lemon rind

1 tablespoon lemon juice

3oz butter

1 medium onion, chopped finely

2 cups arborio rice

¾ cup finely grated parmesan cheese

2 tablespoons finely chopped fresh
  flat-leaf parsley

1 medium lemon, quartered

1 Bring stock and wine to a boil in medium saucepan. Add rind and juice; reduce heat. Cover; keep hot.

2 Heat half of the butter in large saucepan; cook onion, stirring, until soft. Add rice; stir over medium heat until coated in butter mixture .

3 Stir 1 cup of the stock mixture into rice mixture; cook, stirring, over low heat until liquid is absorbed.

4 Continue adding stock mixture in 1-cup batches, stirring after each addition. Total cooking time should be about 35 minutes.

5 Remove pan from heat; serve topped with cheese and parsley. Accompany risotto with lemon quarters.

preparation time 15 minutes cooking time 40 minutes serves 4 per serving 22.1g fat; 668 cal

risotto milanese

3½ cups (875ml) hot chicken stock

½ cup (125ml) dry white wine

¼ teaspoon saffron

2oz butter

1 large onion, chopped finely

1¾ cups arborio rice

2 tablespoons grated parmesan cheese

1 Bring stock, wine and saffron to a boil in medium saucepan. Reduce heat; simmer, covered, while preparing onion and rice.

2 Heat half of the butter in large saucepan; cook onion, stirring until soft. Add rice; stir over medium heat until coated in butter mixture. Stir in 1 cup of the stock mixture; cook, stirring, over low heat until liquid is absorbed.

3 Continue adding stock mixture in 1-cup batches, stirring after each addition until liquid is absorbed. Total cooking time should be about 35 minutes or until rice is tender.

4 Stir in remaining butter and cheese.

preparation time 15 minutes cooking time 40 minutes serves 2 per serving 25.5g fat; 945 cal

gnocchi with burnt butter and sage

3 large red-skinned potatoes (2lbs)

1 clove garlic, crushed

2 tablespoons milk

2 egg yolks

⅓ cup grated parmesan cheese

1 cup flour, approximately

4oz butter, chopped coarsely

12 fresh sage leaves

¼ cup parmesan cheese flakes, extra

freshly ground black pepper

tips A ricer or mouli, available from kitchenware stores, will give the best result for smooth potato.

1 Steam or boil whole unpeeled potatoes until tender; drain. Cool potatoes slightly; peel. Mash potatoes with a ricer, mouli or masher until smooth; stir in garlic and milk. Stir in egg yolks, grated parmesan and enough of the flour to form a firm dough.

2 Roll a quarter of the dough on lightly floured surface into a 1in-thick sausage. Cut into 1in lengths; roll into gnocchi-shaped ovals. Place each oval in palm of hand; press with inverted floured fork tines to flatten gnocchi slightly and make a grooved imprint. Place on lightly floured tray in single layer. Cover; refrigerate 1 hour. [Can be made a day ahead to this stage and refrigerated, covered, or frozen for up to 3 months.]

3 Cook gnocchi, in batches, in large saucepan of boiling water about 3 minutes or until gnocchi float to the surface. Remove from pan with slotted spoon; drain.

4 Meanwhile, cook butter in small shallow frying pan until just browned. Add sage; immediately remove from heat. Divide gnocchi among serving plates; drizzle with sage butter. Serve topped with parmesan flakes, and pepper.

preparation time 25 minutes (plus refrigeration time) cooking time 25 minutes serves 4

per serving 33.2g fat; 591 cal

soft polenta with braised vegetables

2½ cups (625ml) water
1 cup polenta
½ cup finely grated parmesan cheese
1 tablespoon olive oil
1 medium onion, sliced thinly
1 clove garlic, crushed

7oz button mushrooms, halved
2 medium green zucchini (9oz), sliced thickly
8 medium yellow patty-pan squash (4oz), quartered
600ml bottled tomato pasta sauce
¾ cup (180ml) vegetable stock

tips braised vegetables can be prepared in advance and refrigerated, covered; reheat just before serving.
Serve with a tossed green salad and crusty Italian bread, such as ciabatta.

1 Bring the water to a boil in medium saucepan. Sprinkle polenta gradually into the water, stirring constantly. Cover, reduce heat to low; cook, stirring occasionally, about 10 minutes or until polenta thickens. Add cheese, stir until melted.
2 Meanwhile, heat oil in medium saucepan; cook onion and garlic, stirring, until onion softens. Add mushrooms; cook, stirring, 3 minutes. Add zucchini and squash; cook, stirring, 2 minutes. Add sauce and stock; bring to a boil. Reduce heat; simmer, covered, about 8 minutes or until vegetables are just tender.
3 Serve polenta with braised vegetables.
preparation time 15 minutes cooking time 15 minutes serves 4 per serving 10.5g fat; 348 cal

roasted pumpkin and rosemary risotto

2lb 4oz pumpkin, chopped coarsely
¼ cup (60ml) olive oil
1½ cups arborio rice
1 clove garlic, crushed
1 tablespoon fresh rosemary

4 cups hot vegetable stock
5oz baby spinach
¼ cup coarsely grated parmesan cheese
¼ cup (60ml) cream
2 tablespoons parmesan cheese flakes

tip leftover risotto can be made into patties and pan-fried. Serve topped with crisp prosciutto; dot with sour cream.

1 Combine pumpkin and half of the oil in baking dish. Bake, uncovered, at 350º F for about 40 minutes or until pumpkin is tender.
2 Meanwhile, heat remaining oil in large saucepan. Add rice; stir to coat in oil. Add garlic and rosemary; cook, stirring, until fragrant.
3 Stir in 1 cup of the stock; cook, stirring, over low heat until liquid is absorbed.
4 Continue adding stock, in 1-cup batches, stirring after each addition. Total cooking time should be about 35 minutes or until rice is tender; remove from heat.
5 Stir in pumpkin, spinach, grated parmesan and cream. Stir over heat until hot. Serve topped with parmesan flakes.
preparation time 20 minutes cooking time 40 minutes serves 4 per serving 25.3g fat; 591 cal

buttery wine risotto with smoked salmon

6 cups chicken stock
1 cup (250ml) dry white wine
1oz butter
1 medium leek (13oz), chopped finely
2 cloves garlic, crushed
2 cups arborio rice
¼ teaspoon ground turmeric
1oz butter, chopped finely, extra
½ cup finely grated parmesan cheese
4oz smoked salmon, chopped coarsely
2 teaspoons finely chopped fresh dill
2oz baby spinach

1 Bring stock and wine to a boil in medium saucepan; reduce heat. Cover; keep hot.
2 Heat butter in large saucepan; cook leek and garlic, stirring, until leek is very soft. Add rice and turmeric; stir to coat in butter mixture. Stir in 1 cup of the stock mixture; cook, stirring, over low heat until liquid is absorbed.
3 Continue adding stock mixture in 1-cup batches, stirring after each addition. Total cooking time should be about 35 minutes or until rice is tender. Remove pan from heat; stir in extra butter, cheese, salmon, dill and spinach.
preparation time 10 minutes   cooking time 40 minutes   serves 4   per serving   23.1g fat; 672 cal

spinach gnocchi

1lbs 2oz spinach
1¼ cups ricotta cheese
1 cup finely grated parmesan cheese
1 egg, beaten lightly

¼ teaspoon ground nutmeg
flour
2oz butter, melted

1 Steam or microwave spinach until wilted. Rinse under cold running water; drain well. Squeeze as much liquid as possible from spinach; chop finely.

2 Combine spinach, ricotta, half of the parmesan, egg and nutmeg in medium bowl.

3 Using tablespoon and palm of hand, roll mixture into egg shapes.

4 Roll gnocchi lightly in flour. Cook gnocchi, in batches, in large saucepan of boiling water, uncovered, about 3 minutes or until gnocchi float to the surface. Remove from pan with slotted spoon; drain.

5 Arrange gnocchi in ovenproof dish. Pour butter over gnocchi; sprinkle with remaining parmesan. [Can be made a day ahead to this stage and refrigerated, covered; reheat in moderate oven about 20 minutes or until hot.] Cook under moderately hot grill until cheese turns golden brown.

preparation time 30 minutes cooking time 20 minutes serves 4 per serving 25.1g fat; 328 cal

gnocchi alla romana

3 cups (750ml) milk
1½ teaspoons salt
pinch ground nutmeg
⅔ cup semolina

1 egg, beaten lightly
1½ cups grated parmesan cheese
2oz butter, melted

1 Bring milk, salt and nutmeg to a boil in medium saucepan; reduce heat. Gradually add semolina, stirring constantly with wooden spoon.

2 Continue cooking, uncovered, stirring often, about 10 minutes, or until spoon can stand upright in centre. Remove from heat.

3 Combine egg and 1 cup of the cheese in small bowl. Add to semolina mixture; stir well. Spread mixture onto well-oiled 10in x 12in swiss roll pan; using wet spatula smooth until ¼ in thick. Refrigerate about 1 hour or until semolina is firm.

4 Cut semolina into circles using 2in pastry cutter. Arrange circles, overlapping, in greased shallow ovenproof dish. Pour over butter; sprinkle with remaining cheese. Bake in moderate oven about 15 minutes or until crisp and golden.

preparation time 30 minutes (plus refrigerating time) cooking time 40 minutes serves 4
per serving 31.4g fat; 478 cal

polenta

8 cups water
2 teaspoons salt
2 cups polenta
¼ cup (60ml) olive oil

This is a specialty of northern Italy, particularly popular around Venice. Served plain, it is often accompanied by bolognese sauce; or it can be fried and served as an accompaniment to any meat. Hot, fried polenta can also be topped with anchovies and sliced olives or other toppings and served as crostini.

1 Combine the water and salt in large saucepan; bring to a boil. Gradually sprinkle polenta over the water, stirring constantly with wooden spoon; make sure polenta has no lumps.
2 Reduce heat to low, as mixture may bubble and spatter; partially covering the saucepan is a good idea. Continue cooking, stirring, about 30 minutes or until polenta is very thick and spoon can stand upright in centre. [Polenta can be served at this point, piled onto a plate.]
3 Spoon mixture into greased 8in x 12in lamington pan; spread mixture out evenly. Allow to become cold; leave at room temperature a few hours.
4 Turn polenta out of pan; cut into 2in slices. Heat oil in large frying pan until very hot; reduce heat. Gently fry polenta slices until golden brown both sides.
preparation time 15 minutes (plus standing time) cooking time 50 minutes serves 4
per serving 15.4g fat; 400 cal

italian classics

tomato, bocconcini and basil salad

Cut 4 medium tomatoes and 1lb 2oz large bocconcini cheese into ¼in-thick slices. Combine ¼ cup extra virgin olive oil, 2 teaspoons balsamic vinegar, 1 clove crushed garlic and 1 teaspoon caster sugar in screw-top jar; shake well. Layer tomatoes and cheese alternately on serving plate; sprinkle with ¼ cup coarsely chopped fresh basil and dressing.

preparation time 10 minutes serves 6

per serving 21.9g fat; 265 cal

store salad can be made 3 hours ahead and refrigerated, covered.

tip mozzarella can be substituted for the bocconcini; stand 30 minutes before serving.

eggplant and mozzarella slices

Cut 2 medium peeled eggplants into 1in-thick rounds (you will need eight rounds). Split each round in half, horizontally, taking care not to cut all the way through. Gently open out rounds. Cut 9oz mozzarella cheese into eight slices. Place cheese in each of the eggplant rounds. Place 1 basil leaf on each piece of cheese. Fold over eggplant; trim cheese to size of eggplant if necessary. [Can be made 3 hours ahead to this stage and refrigerated, covered.] Heat ¼ cup olive oil in medium frying pan. Cook eggplant over medium heat until browned both sides and tender and cheese begins to melt.

preparation time 15 minutes cooking time 15 minutes serves 8 per serving 13.9g fat; 167 cal

tip thin slices of pancetta can be placed under the cheese.

pears and parmesan

Cut ½ loaf ciabatta into thin slices; brush both sides with 2 tablespoons olive oil. Cook, in batches, on heated oiled grill plate (or grill or barbecue). Wash and peel 6 medium corella pears. Serve with 6oz piece parmesan cheese and ciabatta toast.

preparation time 5 minutes cooking time 5 minutes serves 6 per serving 17.1g fat; 354 cal

tip beurre bosc pears can be substituted for corella pears. Halve or quarter pears; brush cut edges with lemon juice to stop them browning.

figs with prosciutto

Gently break open 4 medium ripe figs. Arrange figs and 8 slices prosciutto on four serving plates. Toss 2oz baby rocket with 2 tablespoons extra virgin olive oil; divide among plates. Sprinkle with salt flakes and ground black pepper, if desired.

preparation time 10 minutes serves 4

per serving 11.1g fat; 145 cal

tip prosciutto is also great served with fresh melon. For a finger food treat, try wrapping cubes of melon in prosciutto, twist the ends like bonbons and serve.

seafood

Italy's extensive coastline and highly developed fishing industry mean that seafood is enjoyed all over the country. Soups, stews and sauces are rich with shellfish of all kinds, lightly fried mixed seafood is a specialty of several regions, and fresh fish is grilled and pan-fried with an almost endless variety of different herbs and flavorings.

slow simmered octopus

2lbs 4oz baby octopus

1 tablespoon olive oil

1 large onion, chopped coarsely

3 cloves garlic, crushed

1 cup (250ml) dry red wine

1lb 14oz canned tomatoes

6 canned anchovy fillets, chopped coarsely

¼ cup tomato paste

¼ cup coarsely chopped fresh oregano

store recipe best made a day ahead, to allow the flavors to develop; can be refrigerated, covered, up to 2 days.

1 Cut heads from octopus just below eyes. Discard heads; remove beaks. Wash octopus; quarter each octopus.

2 Heat oil in large saucepan; cook onion and garlic, stirring, until onion is soft.

3 Add octopus; cook, stirring, until just changed in color.

4 Add wine; cook, stirring, about 5 minutes or until liquid reduces by about a third.

5 Add undrained crushed tomatoes and remaining ingredients; simmer, uncovered, about 1½ hours or until octopus is tender.

preparation time 20 minutes cooking time 1 hour 45 minutes serves 4 per serving 8.1g fat; 326 cal

steamed garlic and herb mussels

80 medium black mussels (4lbs 7oz)

2 tablespoons olive oil

8 cloves garlic, crushed

4 fresh red Thai chilies, seeded, chopped finely

1 tablespoon finely grated lemon rind

1 cup (250ml) lemon juice

1 cup (250ml) dry white wine

½ cup finely chopped fresh flat-leaf parsley

⅓ cup finely chopped fresh basil

1 Scrub mussels; remove beards.

2 Heat oil in large saucepan; cook garlic, chili and rind, stirring, about 2 minutes or until fragrant. Add mussels, juice and wine; bring to a boil. Cook, covered, about 5 minutes or until mussels open (discard any that do not open). Remove mussels from pan.

3 Bring pan liquid to a boil; cook, uncovered, about 10 minutes or until mixture thickens slightly. Stir in parsley and basil.

4 Return mussels to pan; simmer, stirring, until heated through.

preparation time 30 minutes cooking time 25 minutes serves 6 per serving 5.9g fat; 122 cal

squid and crisp prosciutto

2lbs 4oz squid hoods

2 egg whites

1 teaspoon sea salt

1 teaspoon cracked black pepper

vegetable oil, for deep-frying

crisp prosciutto

4oz thinly sliced prosciutto

2 tablespoons brown sugar

1 tablespoon warm water

garlic sauce

2 egg yolks

2 teaspoons lemon juice

2 cloves garlic, crushed

¾ cup (180ml) olive oil

tips cuttlefish can be substituted for the squid hoods.
If sauce is too thick, stir in a teaspoon or two of warm water to thin.

1 Cut squid in half lengthways. Score inside of each piece; cut into 1in-wide strips.

2 Whisk egg whites, salt and pepper in small bowl.

3 Heat oil in large frying pan. Dip squid in egg mixture. Deep-fry, in batches, until squid is tender; drain on absorbent paper.

4 Serve squid with crisp prosciutto and garlic sauce.

crisp prosciutto dip each prosciutto slice in combined sugar and water. Fold in half lengthways; twist into rosette shape. Place on oiled oven tray; bake, uncovered, at 425º F for about 10 minutes or until browned and crisp.

garlic sauce blend or process yolks, juice and garlic until smooth. With motor operating, gradually add oil in thin stream; process until sauce thickens. Transfer to small bowl; refrigerate, covered, until required.

preparation time 15 minutes cooking time 15 minutes serves 4 per serving 62.4g fat; 781 cal

makerel with leek, prosciutto and shrimp

1 medium leek (13oz)
12 large cooked shrimp (9oz)
12 makerel (1lb 13oz), butterflied
12 slices prosciutto

1 cup roasted vegetable pesto
2 medium yellow zucchini (9oz)
2 medium green zucchini (9oz)

tip roasted vegetable pesto is available from most supermarkets; alternatively, you can use your favorite flavored pesto.

1 Cut leek in half lengthways. Cut into 4in lengths; separate layers. Drop leek into medium saucepan of boiling water; drain. Rinse under cold water; drain.

2 Shell and devein shrimp.

3 Flatten makerel with rolling pin. Place fish skin-side down on board; line with pieces of leek, then a slice of prosciutto. Spread each with 1 teaspoon of the pesto; top with a shrimp. Starting from head of fish, roll to enclose shrimp; secure with toothpick. [Can be made a day ahead to this stage and refrigerated, covered.]

4 Cut zucchini lengthways into ¼in-thick slices. Cook on heated oiled grill plate (or grill or barbecue) until browned and tender. Cover; keep warm.

5 Cook fish on grill plate until cooked through. Serve fish with char-grilled zucchini.

preparation time 35 minutes cooking time 15 minutes serves 4 per serving 10g fat; 297 cal

clams with tomato dressing

5lbs 9oz clams, scrubbed
½ cup (125ml) dry white wine
1 small red onion, chopped finely
2 cloves garlic, crushed
2 tablespoons lemon juice

2 tablespoons white wine vinegar
½ cup (125ml) olive oil
5 large tomatoes, chopped coarsely
4 green onions, sliced thinly
2 tablespoons coarsely chopped fresh coriander

1 Rinse clams under cold running water; drain. Place clams in large saucepan with wine. Cover; bring to a boil. Reduce heat; simmer about 5 minutes or until shells open (discard any clams that do not open).

2 Meanwhile, heat large oiled saucepan; cook red onion and garlic over medium heat until browned lightly. Add combined juice, vinegar and oil; cook, stirring, about 2 minutes or until thickened slightly.

3 Drain clams; discard liquid.

4 Gently toss clams with tomato, green onion, coriander and red onion mixture.

preparation time 30 minutes cooking time 10 minutes serves 4 per serving 30.7g fat; 377 cal

snapper with caper and herb crust

1 cup pine nuts
¼ cup rolled oats
¼ cup white sesame seeds
2 cups packaged breadcrumbs
½ teaspoon dry mustard
1 tablespoon grated lemon rind
1 tablespoon lemon juice
1 egg, beaten lightly
1 tablespoon honey
2 tablespoons chopped fresh parsley
2 tablespoons chopped fresh lemon thyme
2 tablespoons drained capers, chopped coarsely
1 cup grated parmesan cheese
8 snapper cutlets (3lbs 6oz)
flour
2 eggs, beaten lightly, extra
½ cup (125ml) vegetable oil

1 Process pine nuts, oats and seeds until chopped finely; transfer to large bowl. Stir in breadcrumbs, mustard, rind, juice, egg, honey, herbs, capers and cheese; mix well. Toss fish in flour; shake away excess. Dip fish in extra egg, then in breadcrumb mixture. [Can be made 3 hours ahead to this stage and refrigerated, covered.]
2 Heat oil in large frying pan; cook fish, in batches, until browned lightly both sides. Transfer to large oven tray; bake, uncovered, in moderate oven about 15 minutes or until cutlets are tender. Serve with lemon wedges and asparagus spears, if desired.

preparation time 20 minutes cooking time 20 minutes serves 8 per serving 40.3g fat; 640 cal

walnut gremolata fish

⅓ cup walnut pieces, toasted,
   chopped finely
2 tablespoons finely chopped lemon rind
¼ cup finely chopped fresh parsley
2 cloves garlic, crushed

4 medium potatoes (1lb 13oz), quartered
1oz butter, chopped coarsely
¼ cup (60ml) milk
4 firm white fish fillets (1lb 7oz)
1 tablespoon olive oil

tip we used bream fillets
for this recipe, but any firm
white fish fillets are suitable.

1 Combine nuts, rind, parsley and half of the garlic in small bowl; cover gremolata.
2 Boil, steam or microwave potato until tender; drain. Mash potato with butter, milk and remaining garlic; keep warm.
3 Meanwhile, brush fish with oil; cook, skin-side down first, on heated oiled grill plate (or grill or barbecue) until browned both sides and cooked through.
4 Serve fish with garlic mash; top with gremolata.

preparation time 25 minutes cooking time 30 minutes serves 4 per serving 24.9g fat; 468 cal

char-grilled seafood salad with gremolata dressing

24 large uncooked shrimp (2lbs 4oz)
1lb 2oz squid hoods
1lb 2oz cleaned baby octopus
1 tablespoon olive oil
1 tablespoon finely chopped lemon rind
1 clove garlic, chopped finely
1 medium green cucumber
4oz mixed sprouts

gremolata dressing
¼ cup (60ml) olive oil
1 tablespoon finely chopped lemon rind
1 clove garlic, chopped finely
2 tablespoons lemon juice
2 tablespoons coarsely chopped fresh
   flat-leaf parsley

1 Shell and devein shrimp, leaving heads and tails intact. Cut squid in half lengthways; score inside surface of each piece. Cut squid into 2in-wide strips. Remove and discard heads from octopus.
2 Combine seafood in large bowl with oil, rind and garlic; refrigerate, covered, until required. [Can be made a day ahead to this stage.]
3 Cook seafood, in batches, on heated oiled grill plate (or grill or barbecue) until shrimp just change color, and squid and octopus are tender.
4 Using vegetable peeler, slice cucumber into ribbons. Combine cucumber with sprouts in medium bowl.
5 Serve seafood on cucumber mixture; drizzle with gremolata dressing.
gremolata dressing combine ingredients in screw-top jar; shake well.

preparation time 30 minutes (plus marinating time) cooking time 20 minutes serves 6
per serving 14.7g fat; 295 cal

fish milanese

1 small onion, chopped finely
2 tablespoons lemon juice
⅓ cup (80ml) olive oil
4 fish fillets
plain flour
2 eggs, beaten lightly
1 tablespoon milk
1 cup packaged breadcrumbs
1 tablespoon olive oil, extra
4oz butter
1 clove garlic, crushed
2 teaspoons finely chopped fresh parsley

1 Combine onion, juice and oil in medium shallow bowl; mix well. Add fish; spoon mixture over fish to coat thoroughly. Cover; refrigerate 1 hour, turning occasionally.
2 Remove fish from marinade. Coat lightly with flour; shake away excess. Combine egg and milk in small bowl; dip fish into egg mixture. Coat in breadcrumbs; press on firmly. [Can be made 3 hours ahead to this stage and refrigerated, covered.]
3 Heat extra oil and half of the butter in large frying pan. Cook fish about 3 minutes each side, or until cooked through; drain on absorbent paper.
4 Heat remaining butter in small saucepan. Cook garlic until butter turns light golden brown; add parsley. Pour browned butter over fish.
preparation time 20 minutes (plus marinating time) cooking time 10 minutes serves 4
per serving 52.4g fat; 620 cal

calamari

1 egg
2 tablespoons milk
2lbs 4oz calamari rings, sliced thinly
2 cups packaged breadcrumbs
vegetable oil for deep-frying

tip calamari can be shallow-fried. Heat a small amount of oil in large frying pan (the oil should reach only halfway up the side of each calamari ring); cook calamari rings in hot oil, about 2 minutes each side, or until golden brown.

1 Beat egg and milk in small bowl. Dip calamari in egg mixture; drain away excess. Toss in breadcrumbs; press breadcrumbs on firmly. [Can be made 3 hours ahead to this stage and refrigerated, covered.]
2 Heat oil in large saucepan. Deep-fry calamari, in batches, about 2 minutes or until golden brown; drain on absorbent paper. Serve with lemon wedges and tartare sauce, if desired.
preparation time 15 minutes cooking time 15 minutes serves 4 per serving 19.2g fat; 351 cal

fritto misto

1lb 2oz uncooked jumbo shrimp
1lb 2oz small squid
9oz white fish fillets
vegetable oil for deep-frying
9oz scallops

batter
1 cup self-raising flour
¼ teaspoon baking soda
pinch salt
1 cup (250ml) water, approximately

1 Shell and devein shrimp, leaving tails intact. Clean squid; cut into thin rings. Cut fish into 2in pieces.
2 Heat oil in large saucepan. Dip shrimps, squid, fish and scallops into batter; drain off excess. Deep-fry seafood in hot oil, in batches, until golden brown. Drain on absorbent paper. Serve hot with tartare sauce, if desired.
batter combine flour, soda and salt in small bowl. Gradually add the water, stirring until batter is smooth. If batter is too thick, add a little more water.
preparation time 35 minutes cooking time 20 minutes serves 6 per serving 17.6g fat; 268 cal

garlic marinated shrimp

2lbs 4oz uncooked jumbo shrimp
¾ cup stale breadcrumbs
6 cloves garlic, crushed
½ cup (125ml) olive oil
freshly ground black pepper
¼ cup (60ml) lemon juice

1 Remove heads from shrimp. Using sharp scissors, cut though shells from head to tail, leaving shells intact. Remove vein from shrimp.
2 Combine breadcrumbs, garlic, oil and enough of the pepper to season, in large bowl. Add shrimp; rub in breadcrumb mixture, trying to get breadcrumbs under shells if possible. Cover; refrigerate 1 hour. [Can be made a day ahead to this stage.]
3 Cook shrimp, in batches, on heated oiled grill plate (or grill or barbecue), until just cooked through. Sprinkle with juice just before serving.
preparation time 30 minutes (plus refrigeration time) cooking time 10 minutes serves 4
per serving 39.8g fat; 415 cal

sardines with tomatoes and caper dressing

16 fresh sardines (1lb 11oz), cleaned

4 medium egg tomatoes (11oz), sliced thickly

1 small red onion, sliced thinly

1 tablespoon coarsely chopped fresh
   flat-leaf parsley

caper dressing

⅓ cup (80ml) red wine vinegar

¼ cup (60ml) extra virgin olive oil

1 tablespoon drained baby capers

1 clove garlic, crushed

1 tablespoon finely chopped fresh parsley

tip have sardines cleaned and the heads removed at the fish monger; they may even butterfly them for you.

1 To butterfly the sardines, cut through the underside of the fish to the tail. Break backbone at tail; peel away backbone. Trim sardines.

2 Cook sardines on heated, oiled grill plate (or grill or barbecue), in batches, until browned both sides and just cooked through. Serve with tomato and onion. Spoon over caper dressing; top with parsley.

caper dressing combine ingredients in screw-top jar; shake well.

preparation time 20 monutes cookign time 10 minutes serves 4 per serving 33.9g fat; 485 cal

fish with chili sherry vinegar

1 tablespoon garlic olive oil

4 cod fillets, skin on (1lb 13oz)

chili sherry vinegar

¼ cup (60ml) garlic olive oil

1½ tablespoons sherry vinegar

1 teaspoon dried chili flakes

2 tablespoons coarsely chopped fresh
   flat-leaf parsley

tip red or white wine vinegar can be substituted for the sherry vinegar.

1 Heat oil in large non-stick frying pan; cook fish, flesh side down, until well browned. Turn fish; cook until browned and just cooked through.

2 Spoon chili sherry vinegar over fish. Serve with lemon wedges and steamed zucchini and beans, if desired.

chili sherry vinegar place oil, vinegar, chili and parsley in clean small saucepan; stir over low heat until just warm—do not overheat.

preparation time 5 minutes cooking time 8 minutes serves 4 per serving 19.7g fat; 317 cal

cioppino

2 uncooked blue swimmer crabs (1lb 9oz)

16 large uncooked shrimp (1lb 2oz)

1lb swordfish steaks

1 tablespoon olive oil

1 medium onion, chopped coarsely

2 trimmed sticks celery, chopped coarsely

3 cloves garlic, crushed

6 medium tomatoes (2lbs 4oz), chopped coarsely

15oz canned tomato purée

½ cup (125ml) dry white wine

1⅓ cups (330ml) fish stock

1 teaspoon sugar

7oz clams, scrubbed

7oz scallops

2 tablespoons finely shredded fresh basil

⅓ cup coarsely chopped fresh flat-leaf parsley

tips substitute any firm-fleshed fish for the swordfish. Originating in San Francisco's large Italian fishing community, cioppino is an Italian-American fish stew.

1 Slip sharp knife under top of crab shell at back; lever off shell. Remove and discard whitish gills. Rinse well under cold running water. Using cleaver, chop each crab into pieces. Shell and devein shrimp, leaving tails intact. Chop fish into 2cm pieces.

2 Heat oil in large saucepan; cook onion, celery and garlic, stirring, until onion is soft. Add tomato; cook, stirring, 5 minutes or until pulpy. Stir in purée, wine, stock and sugar; simmer, covered, 20 minutes.

3 Add crab and clams to pan; simmer, covered, 10 minutes (discard any clams that do not open). Add shrimp, fish and scallops; cook, stirring occasionally, about 5 minutes, or until seafood changes color and is cooked through. Stir in herbs.

preparation time 30 minutes cooking time 45 minutes serves 6 per serving 7.1g fat; 254 cal

pan-fried fish steaks with rosemary and oregano

4 firm white fish steaks (1lb 13oz)
¼ cup (60ml) lemon juice
½ cup (125ml) extra virgin olive oil
1 teaspoon salt
2 teaspoons finely chopped fresh oregano
2 teaspoons finely chopped fresh rosemary

tip we used cod cutlets for this recipe, but any firm white fish cutlets are suitable.

1 Cook fish on heated oiled grill plate (or grill or barbecue) until cooked through; turn once during cooking.
2 Meanwhile, combine remaining ingredients in screw-top jar; shake well.
3 Brush both sides of hot fish with herb dressing; serve with any remaining dressing and patty-pan squash, if desired.
preparation time 5 minutes cooking time 7 minutes serves 4 per serving 32.9g fat; 458 cal

sardines with parmesan crumbs and fresh tomato sauce

16 sardine fillets (9oz)
¼ cup flour
2 tablespoons milk
1 egg
2 cups stale breadcrumbs
1½ cups coarsely grated parmesan cheese
vegetable oil, for shallow-frying

fresh tomato sauce
1 tablespoon olive oil
1 large onion, sliced thinly
2 cloves garlic, crushed
5 medium tomatoes, chopped coarsely
2 teaspoons sugar
⅓ cup (80ml) dry white wine
2 tablespoons coarsely chopped fresh basil

1 Coat fish in flour; shake away excess. Dip fish in combined milk and egg; coat in combined breadcrumbs and cheese. Cover; refrigerate 30 minutes.
2 Heat oil in large frying pan. Shallow-fry fish, in batches, until browned and just cooked through; drain on absorbent paper. Serve fish with fresh tomato sauce; garnish with extra basil, if desired.
fresh tomato sauce heat oil in medium saucepan; cook onion and garlic, stirring, until onion is soft. Add tomato, sugar and wine; simmer, uncovered, about 20 minutes or until sauce thickens. Stir in basil. [Can be made 2 days ahead and refrigerated, covered, or frozen for up to 6 months.]
preparation time 12 minutes (plus refrigeration time) cooking time 30 minutes serves 4
per serving 38.2g fat; 664 cal

shrimp with risotto triangles

24 uncooked shrimp (2lbs 11oz)
½ cup (125ml) olive oil
3 teaspoons finely grated lemon rind
⅓ cup (80ml) lemon juice
½ teaspoon cracked black pepper
2 tablespoons chopped fresh dill
4oz rocket, trimmed

risotto triangles
¼ cup (60ml) olive oil
1 medium onion, chopped finely
1 cup arborio rice
½ cup (125ml) dry white wine
3 cups (750ml) hot vegetable stock
½ cup finely grated parmesan cheese
flour

1 Prepare shrimp; discard heads, leaving meat in shell.

2 Combine oil, rind, juice, pepper and dill in jug. Place shrimp in large bowl; pour over a third
of the marinade.

3 Cook shrimp in heated large saucepan, stirring, about 3 minutes or until cooked through. Serve
shrimp, on rocket, with risotto triangles; drizzle with reserved marinade.

risotto triangles coat 9in-square slab cake pan with cooking-oil spray; line base and two sides
with baking paper, extending paper 1in above edge of pan. Heat 1 tablespoon of the oil in medium
saucepan; cook onion, stirring, until soft. Add rice; stir to coat with oil. Add wine; cook, stirring, until
wine is absorbed. Stir in stock; cook, uncovered, stirring occasionally, about 20 minutes or until rice
is just tender and liquid is absorbed. Stir in cheese; press risotto into prepared pan. Cover; refrigerate
3 hours or overnight. Cut risotto into four squares; cut each square into four triangles. Coat triangles in
flour; shake off excess. Heat remaining oil in large saucepan; cook risotto triangles, in batches, until
browned both sides and heated through. Drain on absorbent paper.

preparation time 30 minutes (plus refrigeration time) cooking time 50 minutes serves 4
per serving 51g fat; 871 cal

meat

While Italy both produces and enjoys excellent beef, lamb, and pork, it is nonetheless veal dishes for which the country is justifiably most famous—melt-in-the-mouth scallopini and Milan's famous osso buco. But veal is only part of the story, with all kinds of delicious and authentic meat dishes in the following pages.

vitello tonnato

3lbs 6oz nut of veal
2oz canned flat anchovy fillets, drained
1 clove garlic, sliced thinly
2 medium carrots, chopped finely
3 trimmed sticks celery, chopped finely
2 medium onions, quartered
6 sprigs parsley
5 cups chicken stock

1½ cups (375ml) dry white wine
1½ tablespoons capers
tuna sauce
¾ cup (180ml) vegetable oil
1 egg yolk
4oz canned tuna, drained
2 tablespoons lemon juice
¼ cup (60ml) cream

1 Using tip of sharp knife, make shallow cuts along length of veal. Cut four anchovy fillets into ½in lengths; reserve remaining anchovies. Insert anchovy pieces and garlic into each cut in veal. Place veal in large saucepan; cover with cold water. Bring to a boil; boil 1 minute, uncovered. Drain veal; rinse under cold running water.
2 Return veal to pan with carrot, celery, onion, parsley, stock and wine; bring to a boil. Reduce heat; simmer, partly covered, about 1½ hours or until veal is tender. Remove veal from stock; leave to cool. Reserve ¼ cup stock for sauce; cool. [Can be made a day ahead to this stage and refrigerated, covered.]
3 Cut veal into thin slices. Dip veal into sauce and arrange in overlapping slices around plate. Serve remainder of sauce separately; sprinkle with capers.
tuna sauce cover reserved anchovy fillets with water; stand 10 minutes. Drain; pat dry with absorbent paper. Place oil, egg yolk, tuna, anchovy and juice in blender; blend until smooth. Place mixture in small bowl; stir in cream and reserved stock. [Can be made a day ahead and refrigerated, covered.]
preparation time 40 minutes cooking time 1 hour 30 minutes (plus cooling time) serves 6
per serving 39.4g fat; 663 cal

veal scallopini

4 veal cutlets (11oz)
1oz butter
1 small onion, chopped finely
¼ cup (60ml) dry sherry

2 teaspoons flour
½ cup (125ml) beef stock
4oz button mushrooms, sliced thinly
2 tablespoons cream

1 Remove fat from veal; pound veal out thinly.
2 Melt butter in large frying pan; cook veal, while butter is foaming, about 3 minutes, turning once. Remove from pan; cook onion until soft. Pour in sherry.
3 Bring sherry to a boil. Stir in blended flour and stock; stir until sauce comes to a boil.
4 Return veal to pan. Add mushrooms; mix well. Cover pan; simmer gently 10 minutes. Stir in cream; stir until heated through.
preparation time 10 minutes cooking time 20 minutes serves 4 per serving 13.8g fat; 287 cal

braised pork with fresh sage

3oz butter

3lbs 6oz rack of pork (6 cutlets)

2 medium carrots, sliced thickly

6 baby onions, peeled

4 cloves garlic, peeled

2 bay leaves

6 sprigs fresh thyme

1⅓ cups (330ml) dry white wine

fresh sage sauce

1oz butter

1 tablespoon flour

1 tablespoon fresh sage

tips ask your butcher to remove rind and tie pork well.
Roast salted rind on rack in hot oven until crisp; serve with the pork.

1 Melt butter in large flameproof dish; cook pork until browned each side. Remove pork from dish. Place carrot, onion, garlic, bay leaves and thyme in dish; stir over heat about 5 minutes or until just browned. Return pork to dish with wine; transfer to 350° F oven for about 1¼ hours or until tender. Remove pork; keep warm.

2 Strain cooking liquid; reserve liquid. Discard vegetables.

3 Serve pork with sage sauce, roasted tomatoes and potatoes, if desired.

fresh sage sauce bring reserved liquid to a boil in medium saucepan; whisk in blended butter and flour. Boil, whisking constantly, until thickened slightly; stir in sage.

preparation time 15 minutes cooking time 1 hour 30 minutes serves 6 per serving 35.6g fat; 489 cal

meatballs with chili mushroom sauce

1lb 2oz ground pork and veal	1 egg, beaten lightly
1 cup stale breadcrumbs	1 tablespoon olive oil
¼ cup finely chopped fresh oregano	9oz button mushrooms, sliced thinly
3 cloves garlic, crushed	1lb 14oz canned tomatoes
⅓ cup tomato paste	¼ cup (60ml) mild chili sauce

store recipe can be made 2 days ahead and refrigerated, covered, or frozen for up to 3 months.

1 Combine ground meat, breadcrumbs, oregano, garlic, paste and egg in medium bowl; roll level tablespoons of mixture into balls. Place meatballs on oiled oven tray; bake, uncovered, at 400° F for about 15 minutes or until cooked through.

2 Meanwhile, heat oil in large saucepan; cook mushrooms, stirring, until just soft. Add undrained crushed tomatoes and chili sauce to pan; bring to a boil. Reduce heat; simmer, uncovered, 5 minutes. Add meatballs; cook, stirring, 2 minutes.

preparation time 15 minutes cooking time 20 minutes serves 4 per serving 16.4g fat; 393 cal

rib eye steak with roasted vegetables

2 medium red peppers (14oz)
2 small eggplants (1lb)
2 medium zucchini (9oz)
6 beef rib eye steaks (2lbs 14oz)
2 tablespoons olive oil
⅓ cup (60ml) olive paste

tip recipe best made just before serving.

1 Quarter peppers; remove and discard seeds and membranes. Roast peppers under grill or in 475° F oven, skin side up, until skin blisters and blackens. Cover capsicum pieces in plastic or paper 5 minutes. Peel away skin; slice thickly. Cut eggplants into 1in slices. Cut zucchini, lengthways, into 1in slices.

2 Cook steaks, in batches, on heated oiled grill plate (or grill or barbecue) until browned both sides and cooked as desired. Cover to keep warm. Heat oil on grill plate; cook pepper, eggplant and zucchini, in batches, until browned all over and soft.

3 Top steaks with pepper, eggplant, zucchini and olive paste; drizzle with a little extra olive oil, if desired.

preparation time 10 minutes cooking time 1 hour 20 minutes serves 6 per serving 21.8g fat; 450 cal

osso buco

3oz butter

2 medium carrots, chopped finely

2 large brown onions, chopped finely

3 trimmed sticks celery, chopped finely

2 cloves garlic, crushed

16 pieces veal shin or osso buco (4lbs 7oz)

plain flour

2 tablespoons olive oil

1lb 13oz canned tomatoes

½ cup (125ml) dry red wine

1¾ cups (430ml) beef stock

1 tablespoon finely chopped fresh basil

1 teaspoon finely chopped fresh thyme

1 bay leaf

1in strip lemon rind

¼ cup finely chopped fresh parsley

1 teaspoon grated lemon rind

tip the traditional accompaniment for osso buco is risotto milanese (page 105).

1 Heat a third of the butter (1oz) in large saucepan; cook carrot, onion, celery and half of the garlic until onion is golden brown. Remove from heat; transfer vegetables to large ovenproof dish.

2 Coat veal with flour. Heat remaining butter and oil in pan. Add veal; brown well each side. Carefully pack veal on top of vegetables.

3 Drain away fat from pan. Add undrained crushed tomatoes, wine, stock, basil, thyme, bay leaf and strip of lemon rind; bring sauce to a boil.

4 Pour sauce over veal. Cover casserole; bake in 350º F oven for about 1½ hours or until veal is very tender, stirring occasionally. To serve, sprinkle with combined remaining garlic, parsley and grated lemon rind.

preparation time 30 minutes cooking time 2 hours serves 6 per serving 9.6g fat; 404 cal

pepper steaks with balsamic browned onion

1 teaspoon cracked black pepper

2 tablespoons finely chopped fresh parsley

4 beef sirloin steaks (1lb 13oz)

¼ cup (60ml) olive oil

2 large onions, sliced thinly

2 tablespoons balsamic vinegar

1 tablespoon drained, chopped sun-dried tomatoes in oil

2 cloves garlic, crushed

1 Press pepper and parsley onto beef; stand, covered, while cooking onions.

2 Heat 1 tablespoon of the oil in large frying pan; cook onions, stirring, about 10 minutes or until just browned. Add 1 tablespoon of the vinegar; cook, stirring, further 5 minutes or until onion caramelizes. Remove from pan; cover to keep warm. Combine remaining oil and vinegar in small screw-top jar with tomatoes and garlic; shake well.

3 Cook beef on heated oiled grill plate (or grill or barbecue) until browned both sides and cooked as desired. Serve beef with browned onions and tomato dressing.

preparation time 10 minutes cooking time 20 minutes serves 4 per serving 28g fat; 449 cal

braciole with cheese

8 beef minute steaks (2lbs 11oz)

4 cloves garlic, crushed

8 slices prosciutto

7oz smoked provolone, cut into 8 slices

¾ cup stale breadcrumbs

flour

¼ cup (60ml) olive oil

1 medium white onion, sliced thinly

15oz canned tomatoes

1 cup (250ml) water

2 tablespoons tomato paste

¼ cup (60ml) red wine

store recipe best made a day ahead; can be refrigerated, covered, up to 3 days, or frozen for up to 3 months.
Reheat at 325° F for about 45 minutes or until hot.

1 Place beef out flat on clean surface. Spread garlic over each piece. Top each with a slice of prosciutto and a slice of cheese. Place 1 tablespoon of the breadcrumbs in centre of each piece. Roll up beef to enclose filling; secure with string. Toss rolls in flour; shake away excess.

2 Heat oil in large saucepan; cook beef rolls until well browned all over. Remove from pan. Cook onion in same pan, over low heat until very soft. Stir in undrained crushed tomatoes, the water, paste and wine. Bring to a boil; reduce heat. Simmer, covered, 20 minutes.

3 Remove lid; remove beef rolls to pan. Simmer, uncovered, 15 minutes or until sauce thickens slightly. Remove string before serving.

preparation time 30 minutes cooking time 1 hour 45 minutes serves 4 per serving 48.6g fat; 850 cal

pot roast lamb calabrese with creamed polenta

2 medium red peppers (14oz)
2 medium yellow peppers (14oz)
¼ cup (60ml) olive oil
3lbs 6oz lamb neck fillet roasts
2 medium onions, sliced thickly
3 cloves garlic, crushed
15oz canned tomatoes
1 cup (250ml) dry red wine
2 tablespoons lamb or chicken stock
2 tablespoons tomato paste
1 tablespoon finely chopped fresh oregano

creamed polenta
5 cups water
1¼ cups polenta
2oz butter
½ cup coarsely grated parmesan cheese
¾ cup (180ml) cream
¼ cup (60ml) chicken stock

tip lamb neck fillet roasts have to be ordered from your butcher; ask that the lamb be tied securely.

1 Halve peppers; remove and discard seeds and membranes. Cut each half into four equal-sized slices.
2 Heat half of the oil in large frying pan; cook lamb, in batches, until browned lightly. Heat remaining oil in pan; cook onion, garlic and pepper, stirring, until onion is soft.
3 Return lamb to pan with undrained crushed tomatoes and remaining ingredients; bring to a boil. Reduce heat; simmer, covered, 1½ hours. Uncover; simmer further 1 hour. Remove lamb from pan. Remove and discard string; cover lamb to keep warm.
4 Bring tomato mixture in pan to a boil; reduce heat. Simmer, uncovered, about 20 minutes or until tomato mixture thickens. Return lamb to pan. [Can be made 2 days ahead to this stage and refrigerated, covered.]
5 Serve lamb and tomato mixture with creamed polenta.
creamed polenta bring the water to a boil in large saucepan; reduce heat. Gradually whisk in polenta; cook, stirring, over medium heat, 30 minutes. Stir in remaining ingredients until heated through; serve immediately.
preparation time 10 minutes cooking time 2 hours serves 6 per serving 41.5g fat; 802 cal

pork steaks with baked pepper salad

4 pork butterfly steaks (1lb 5oz)
½ teaspoon cracked black pepper
½ teaspoon dried oregano
2 teaspoons olive oil
1 teaspoon cornstarch
1 cup (250ml) chicken stock
2 teaspoons red wine vinegar

baked pepper salad
2 medium yellow peppers (14oz)
2 large tomatoes, halved
3oz button mushrooms, sliced thinly
4 cloves garlic, crushed
¼ teaspoon dried oregano
2 teaspoons olive oil
16 pitted black olives
2 tablespoons grated parmesan cheese

store recipe can be made a day ahead and refrigerated, covered.

1 Sprinkle pork with pepper and oregano. Heat oil in large frying pan; cook pork, until tender, turning once. Remove from pan.

2 Add blended cornstarch and stock to pan; stir until mixture boils and thickens. Add vinegar; return pork to pan. Turn to coat in sauce.

3 Serve with baked pepper salad. Sprinkle with fresh oregano, if desired.

baked pepper salad quarter peppers; remove seeds and membranes. Place pepper on oiled oven tray with tomato, mushrooms and garlic; sprinkle with oregano and oil. Bake, uncovered, at 400º F for 40 minutes. Add olives; sprinkle cheese over tomato. Bake further 15 minutes or until pepper is tender.

preparation time 20 minutes cooking time 1 hour 10 minutes serves 4 per serving 11.7g fat; 295 cal

calves liver with lemon and capers

1lb 2oz calves liver
1 tablespoon olive oil
2oz butter
¼ cup (60ml) lemon juice

½ teaspoon sugar
1 tablespoon baby capers
1 tablespoon fresh flat-leaf parsley leaves

tip ask your butcher to slice the liver thinly for you.

1 Slice liver thinly; remove any membrane.

2 Heat oil and half of the butter in large frying pan. Cook liver quickly, over high heat, until browned all over and cooked as desired; remove from pan.

3 Add juice, sugar and remaining butter to pan; stir over medium heat until butter melts. Return liver to pan with capers and parsley. Cook, turning liver, until well coated and heated through.

preparation time 10 minutes cooking time 10 minutes serves 4 per serving 27.6g fat; 366 cal

veal parmesan

4 veal steaks (11oz)

flour

1 egg

1 tablespoon water

packaged breadcrumbs

1oz butter

⅓ cup (80ml) olive oil

2½ cups grated mozzarella cheese

¾ cup grated parmesan cheese

tomato sauce

1 tablespoon olive oil

1 medium onion, chopped finely

1 trimmed stick celery, chopped finely

1 medium red pepper, chopped finely

1 clove garlic, crushed

15oz canned tomatoes

2 teaspoons sugar

1 tablespoon tomato paste

1½ cups (375ml) chicken stock

1 tablespoon finely chopped fresh parsley

1 tablespoon finely chopped fresh basil

1 Pound veal out thinly. Toss veal in flour; shake off excess. Dip in combined beaten egg and water; press on breadcrumbs. Refrigerate veal while preparing tomato sauce.

2 Heat butter and half of the oil in large frying pan; cook veal until browned both sides. Place in ovenproof dish; top veal with mozzarella. Spoon tomato sauce over mozzarella.

3 Sprinkle evenly with parmesan; drizzle with remaining oil. Bake, uncovered, at 350º F for about 20 minutes or until golden brown.

tomato sauce heat oil in medium frying pan; cook onion, celery, pepper and garlic, stirring until onion is soft. Push tomatoes with their liquid through sieve. Add pureed tomato to pan with sugar, paste and stock. Cover; bring to a boil. Reduce heat; simmer, covered, 30 minutes. Remove lid; simmer until sauce is thick. Stir through parsley and basil.

preparation time 35 minutes cooking time 1 hour 20 minutes serves 4 per serving 52.8g fat; 790 cal

poultry & game

Chicken is as popular in Italy as it is in other countries. But whether it is pan-fried with a simple sauce or transformed into a country-style casserole, the flavors are still Italian. There are also recipes for quail, duck and rabbit as these robust dishes, of largely peasant origin, are also widely popular.

chicken, lemon and artichoke skewers

3 medium lemons

2 cloves garlic, crushed

¼ cup (60ml) olive oil

1lb 5oz chicken breast fillets, chopped coarsely

1lb 13oz can artichoke hearts, drained, halved

24 button mushrooms

1 Squeeze juice from one lemon (you will need two tablespoons of juice). Combine juice, garlic and oil in small screw-top jar; shake well.

2 Cut remaining lemons into 24 wedges. Thread chicken, artichoke, mushrooms and lemon onto 12 skewers. [Can be made a day ahead to this stage and refrigerated, covered.]

3 Cook skewers on heated oiled grill plate (or grill or barbecue) until browned all over and cooked through. Brush with oil mixture during cooking.

preparation time 20 minutes cooking time 10 minutes serves 4 per serving 22.6g fat; 365 cal

chicken marsala

2oz butter

1 clove garlic, crushed

4 single chicken breast fillets (1lb 8oz)

4 slices mozzarella cheese

12 capers, drained

4 anchovy fillets, drained

1 tablespoon finely chopped fresh parsley

¼ cup (60ml) marsala

⅔ cup (160ml) cream

1 Melt butter in large frying pan. Cook garlic and chicken until browned both sides; remove from pan. Arrange one slice of the cheese, three capers and one anchovy fillet on each chicken fillet; sprinkle with parsley.

2 Return chicken to pan; cover. Cook over moderate heat until chicken is cooked through; remove from pan. Place on serving dish; keep warm.

3 Add marsala to pan; scrape brown bits off bottom of pan. Reduce heat; add cream. Simmer gently, uncovered, a few minutes until sauce thickens. Spoon sauce over chicken.

preparation time 15 minutes cooking time 15 minutes serves 4 per serving 44.8g fat; 615 cal

quail with polenta

8 quail (3lbs 9oz)

2 teaspoons olive oil

5 slices pancetta, chopped coarsely

1 tablespoon pine nuts

¼ cup (60ml) brandy

¼ cup raisins

1¾ cups (430ml) chicken stock

marinade

½ cup (125ml) olive oil

1 tablespoon coarsely chopped fresh rosemary

2 teaspoons coarsely chopped fresh thyme

1 tablespoon finely shredded lemon rind

polenta

1½ cups (375ml) chicken stock

½ cup polenta

1oz butter, melted

¼ cup grated parmesan cheese

2 tablespoons polenta, extra

olive oil for shallow-frying

1 Remove and discard necks from quail. Using kitchen scissors, cut through either side of backbone; discard backbone. Cut quail in half. Rinse quail under cold running water; pat dry with absorbent paper.

2 Place quail in large shallow glass or china dish. Pour over marinade; refrigerate, covered, 3 hours. [Can be made a day ahead to this stage.]

3 Heat oil in large frying pan; cook drained quail, in batches, covered, 5 minutes. Turn quail; cook, covered, further 7 minutes or until well browned and tender. Keep warm in 350º F oven.

4 Add pancetta and pine nuts to pan; cook, stirring, 2 minutes or until pine nuts are browned lightly. Add brandy and raisins; cook 2 minutes or until liquid reduces by half. Add stock; simmer, uncovered, about 5 minutes or until thickened slightly.

5 Serve quail with polenta and sauce.

marinade combine ingredients in small bowl; mix well.

polenta bring stock to a boil in large saucepan. Gradually add polenta; simmer, stirring, about 10 minutes or until soft and thick. Stir in butter and cheese. Press firmly into oiled 7in sandwich cake pan; cool. Refrigerate, covered, 3 hours. [Can be made a day ahead to this stage.] Turn cooked polenta out of pan; cut into wedges. Coat wedges in extra polenta. Heat oil in medium frying pan; shallow-fry polenta wedges until browned lightly.

preparation time 25 minutes (plus refrigeration time)   cooking time 55 minutes   serves 4
per serving 87.7g fat; 1159 cal

chicken osso buco

8 chicken thigh cutlets (2lbs 14oz)

¼ cup flour

2 tablespoons olive oil

1 large leek (1lb 2oz), sliced thickly

2 cloves garlic, crushed

2 tablespoons tomato paste

2½ cups (625ml) chicken stock

½ cup (125ml) dry white wine

14oz canned tomatoes

3 trimmed sticks celery, chopped coarsely

2 medium carrots, chopped coarsely

gremolata

1 medium lemon

¼ cup finely chopped fresh parsley

2 cloves garlic, chopped finely

1 Remove and discard skin from chicken. Reserve 1 tablespoon of the flour. Toss chicken in remaining flour; shake off excess. Heat half of the oil in large saucepan; cook chicken, in batches, until browned all over.

2 Heat remaining oil in pan; cook leek and garlic, stirring, until leek is soft. Add reserved flour and paste; cook, stirring, 1 minute. Stir in stock, wine and undrained crushed tomatoes; bring to a boil.

3 Return chicken to pan. Reduce heat; simmer, covered, 1¼ hours. Add celery and carrot; simmer, uncovered, 20 minutes or until vegetables are soft. [Can be made a day ahead to this stage and refrigerated, covered.]

4 Just before serving, sprinkle with gremolata.

gremolata using vegetable peeler, remove rind from lemon. Cut rind into thin strips; chop finely. Combine lemon, parsley and garlic in small bowl; mix well.

preparation time 25 minutes cooking time 1 hour 45 minutes serves 4 per serving 15.6g fat; 469 cal

chicken pancetta casserole

4lbs 7oz chicken thigh cutlets

2 tablespoons olive oil

12 slices pancetta

2 medium onions, sliced thinly

2 cloves garlic, crushed

1lb 14oz canned tomatoes

⅓ cup tomato paste

1 cup (250ml) dry white wine

2 cups (500ml) chicken stock

2 medium carrots, chopped coarsely

⅓ cup finely chopped fresh flat-leaf parsley

1 Remove and discard skin from chicken.

2 Heat half of the oil in large saucepan; cook chicken, in batches, until browned all over.

3 Cut pancetta slices in half. Heat remaining oil in pan; cook onion, garlic and pancetta, stirring, until pancetta is browned.

4 Return chicken to pan with undrained crushed tomatoes, paste, wine and stock; bring to a boil. Reduce heat; simmer, uncovered, 30 minutes. Add carrot; simmer about 30 minutes or until carrot is tender. [Can be made a day ahead to this stage and refrigerated, covered, or frozen for up to 2 months.]

5 Stir through parsley just before serving. Serve with tiny new potatoes, if desired.

preparation time 25 minutes   cooking time 1 hour 20 minutes serves 8 per serving 20.8g fat; 400 cal

chicken cacciatore

2 tablespoons olive oil

3lbs 6oz chicken pieces

1 medium onion, chopped finely

1 clove garlic, crushed

½ cup (125ml) dry white wine

1½ tablespoons vinegar

½ cup (125ml) chicken stock

15oz canned tomatoes

1 tablespoon tomato paste

1 teaspoon finely chopped fresh basil

1 teaspoon sugar

3 anchovy fillets, chopped finely

¼ cup (60ml) milk

2oz pitted black olives, halved

1 tablespoon finely chopped fresh parsley

1 Heat oil in large frying pan; cook chicken until browned all over. Place chicken in ovenproof dish.
2 Pour off most pan juices, leaving about 1 tablespoon in pan. Add onion and garlic to pan; cook until onion is soft. Add wine and vinegar; bring to a boil. Boil until reduced by half. Add stock; stir over high heat 2 minutes. Push tomatoes with their liquid through sieve; add to pan with paste, basil and sugar. Cook further 1 minute.
3 Pour tomato mixture over chicken pieces. Cover; cook at 350º F for 1 hour.
4 Soak anchovy in milk 5 minutes; drain on absorbent paper. Arrange chicken pieces on serving dish; keep warm. Pour pan juices into medium saucepan. Bring to a boil; boil 1 minute. Add anchovy, olives and parsley to pan; cook 1 minute. Pour sauce over chicken pieces. Sprinkle with extra chopped parsley, if desired.
preparation time 30 minutes cooking time 1 hour 20 minutes serves 4 per serving 42.2g fat; 612 cal

rabbit with rosemary and white wine

2 rabbits (4lbs 7oz)
¼ cup (60ml) olive oil
1 medium leek (13oz), sliced thinly
2 trimmed sticks celery, chopped finely
2 cloves garlic, crushed
¼ cup flour

2½ cups (625ml) chicken stock
½ cup (125ml) dry white wine
1 tablespoon fresh rosemary
7oz button mushrooms
2 medium zucchini (7oz), sliced thinly
1 tablespoon finely chopped fresh parsley

store recipe can be made a day ahead and refrigerated, covered, or frozen for up to 3 months.

1 Clean and trim rabbits; cut into pieces. Rinse under cold water; pat dry with absorbent paper.

2 Heat 1 tablespoon of the oil in large frying pan. Cook rabbit, in batches, until browned all over; drain on absorbent paper. Heat remaining oil in pan; cook leek, celery and garlic, stirring, until leek is soft.

3 Stir in flour; stir until mixture is dry and grainy. Remove pan from heat; gradually stir in stock and wine. Stir over heat until mixture boils and thickens. Return rabbit to pan; add rosemary. Simmer, covered, about 1½ hours or until rabbit is tender.

4 Add vegetables; simmer, covered, 20 minutes or until vegetables are tender. Stir in parsley.

preparation time 20 minutes cooking time 2 hours 10 minutes serves 4 per serving 32g fat; 852 cal

chicken parmesan with basil dressing

2 cups stale breadcrumbs
⅓ cup finely grated parmesan cheese
2 tablespoons finely chopped fresh
    flat-leaf parsley
12 chicken tenderloins (1lb 11oz)
¾ cup flour
2 eggs, beaten lightly
9oz curly endive
5oz rocket

basil dressing
1 cup firmly packed fresh basil
½ cup (125ml) olive oil
¼ cup (60ml) lemon juice
1 clove garlic, crushed

tips make breadcrumbs from any stale bread (sourdough or ciabatta are both good). When blending or processing bread to make breadcrumbs, add parmesan and parsley at the very end of processing time, pulsing just a few times to combine the three ingredients thoroughly.

1 Combine breadcrumbs, cheese and parsley in medium bowl.

2 Toss chicken in flour to coat; shake away excess. Dip in egg, then in breadcrumb mixture to coat. Place on oiled oven trays. [Can be made a day ahead to this stage and refrigerated, covered, or frozen for up to 2 months.]

3 Bake at 400° F, uncovered, about 20 minutes or until browned lightly and cooked through.

4 Serve chicken with endive and rocket; drizzle with basil dressing.

basil dressing blend or process ingredients until combined. [Dressing can be made a day ahead and refrigerated, covered.]

preparation time 25 minutes cooking time 20 minutes serves 4 per serving 43.8g fat; 753 cal

slow-roasted duck with sage and rosemary

2 tablespoons finely chopped fresh sage

2 tablespoons finely chopped fresh rosemary

2 teaspoons salt

6 cloves garlic, crushed

2 tablespoons olive oil

3lbs 9oz duck

3 medium white onions, chopped coarsely

2 medium carrots, chopped coarsely

3 medium tomatoes, chopped coarsely

1 cup (250ml) red wine

½ cup (125ml) chicken stock

tip serve with creamy whipped potatoes and lots of fresh bread to mop up the sauce.

1 Combine herbs, salt, garlic and half of the oil in small bowl.

2 Wash duck under cold running water; remove and discard fat from inside cavity. Pat duck dry with absorbent paper. Place half of the onion inside cavity of duck. Loosen skin of duck by sliding fingers between skin and meat at the neck joint; spread half of the herb mixture under skin evenly. Tuck wings under duck; tie legs together with kitchen string.

3 Heat remaining oil in large flameproof baking dish; cook remaining onion, carrot and tomato, stirring, until tomato begins to soften. Add wine and stock to dish; bring to a boil. Remove from heat; stir in remaining herb mixture.

4 Place duck on top of vegetable mixture. Bake tightly covered, at 275° F for 3½ hours, basting with juices several times during cooking.

5 Carefully remove duck from dish and place on oven tray. Return to oven; bake, uncovered, about 30 minutes or until skin is crisp and golden.

6 Meanwhile, strain pan contents into medium saucepan; discard vegetables. Blot the top of pan juices with absorbent paper to remove as much fat as possible. Reheat pan juices and serve over duck.

preparation time 30 minutes cooking time 4 hours serves 4 per serving 93.8g fat; 1055 cal

grandmother's chicken

2 tablespoons vegetable oil

1 large onion, sliced thickly

2 cloves garlic, crushed

4 chicken thigh cutlets (1lb 7oz)

4 chicken drumsticks (1lb 5oz)

4 sprigs fresh rosemary

4 medium potatoes (1lb 13oz), chopped

2 medium tomatoes, chopped coarsely

½ cup (125ml) chicken stock

5oz button mushrooms, halved

4 bacon slices, chopped coarsely

½ cup kalamata black olives

store recipe can be made 2 days ahead and refrigerated, covered, or frozen for up to 2 months.

1 Heat oil in large flameproof baking dish; cook onion and garlic, stirring, until onion is soft. Add chicken; cook, stirring, until just browned all over. Add rosemary, potato, tomato and stock.

2 Bake, uncovered, at 425º F for 1 hour. Stir in mushrooms, bacon and olives. Bake, uncovered, about 20 minutes or until chicken is tender.

preparation time 15 minutes cooking time 1 hour 30 minutes serves 4 per serving 45.5g fat; 742 cal

char-grilled chicken with broad beans and chive butter

1lb 11oz broad beans, shelled

1 tablespoon olive oil

1 small red onion, sliced thinly

2 cloves garlic, crushed

2 medium tomatoes, chopped coarsely

2 tablespoons coarsely chopped fresh parsley

4 single chicken breast fillets (1lb 8oz)

chive butter

2oz butter

2 tablespoons fresh chives

1 Boil, steam or microwave beans until tender; cool. Remove and discard grey skins.

2 Heat oil in medium frying pan; cook onion, covered, over low heat until very soft and starting to caramelise. Add garlic and beans; stir until heated through. Stir in tomato and parsley; stir over low heat 5 minutes.

3 Meanwhile, cook chicken on heated oiled grill plate (or grill or barbecue) about 5 minutes or until cooked though; turn once during cooking.

4 Serve chicken on bean mixture; top with chive butter.

chive butter combine butter and chives in small bowl.

preparation time 15 minutes cooking time 20 minutes serves 4 per serving 27g fat; 453 cal

frittata

tips frittata can be cooked on top of the stove, in a medium lightly oiled slightly-sided frying pan; cook on low heat, uncovered, until almost set, then brown frittata under a preheated grill.
Frittata can be served hot or cold.

salami, potato and basil

Grease deep 8in-round cake pan; line base and side with baking paper. Boil, steam or microwave 2 medium thinly sliced potatoes until just tender. Drain; cool. Cook 9oz finely chopped italian salami in small heated frying pan, stirring, until salami is browned all over; drain on absorbent paper. Layer half of the potato over base of prepared pan; top with half of the salami. Repeat with remaining potato and salami. Combine 6 lightly beaten eggs, ½ cup cream, 3 coarsely chopped green onions and 1 tablespoon finely shredded fresh basil in bowl; pour over potato mixture. Bake at 350º F for 30 minutes or until firm.
preparation time 10 minutes cooking time 45 minutes (plus cooling time) serves 4 per serving 45.1g fat; 569 cal

onion and zucchini

Brush base and sides of deep 8in-square cake pan with 1oz melted butter. Heat 2 tablespoons olive oil in medium frying pan. Cook 2 medium thinly sliced brown onions, stirring, until soft; cool. Combine onion, 6 lightly beaten eggs, ¼ cup cream, ¾ cup grated parmesan cheese, 2 small thinly sliced zucchini and 1 tablespoon finely shredded fresh basil in medium bowl. Pour mixture into prepared pan; bake at 350º F for 25 minutes or until browned lightly and firm.
preparation time 10 minutes cooking time 30 minutes (plus cooling time) serves 4 per serving 13g fat; 160 cal

rocket and prosciutto

Grease deep 8in-square cake pan; line base and two opposite sides with baking paper. Cook 8 slices prosciutto, in batches, in medium heated frying pan until browned all over and crisp; drain on absorbent paper. Place half of the prosciutto in prepared pan; cover with 1oz rocket leaves, then ¼ cup finely grated parmesan cheese. Repeat with remaining prosciutto, another 1oz rocket leaves and ¼ cup finely grated parmesan cheese. Combine 10 lightly beaten eggs and ¾ cup cream into bowl; pour into pan, pressing down on prosciutto mixture to cover completely with egg mixture. Bake at 350º F for 30 minutes or until firm; stand 5 minutes. Turn out of pan; cut into eight pieces.
preparation time 15 minutes cooking time 35 minutes (plus cooling time) serves 4 per serving 25.3g fat; 327 cal

tuna and asparagus

Boil, steam or microwave 5 medium thinly sliced potatoes until almost tender. Cook 1 medium thinly sliced brown onion and 1 clove crushed garlic in small heated frying pan, stirring, until onion softens. Combine potato and onion mixture in large bowl with 9oz coarsely chopped trimmed asparagus, 15oz drained canned tuna, 8 lightly beaten eggs and 2 tablespoons finely chopped fresh flat-leaf parsely. Reheat pan; remove from heat. Spray lightly with cooking-oil spray; return to heat. Spoon frittata mixture into pan; press down firmly. Cook, uncovered, over low heat until almost set; remove from heat. Place under heated grill until frittata sets and top is browned lightly.
preparation time 10 minutes cooking time 30 minutes serves 4 per serving 13.9g fat; 442 cal

salads & vegetables

From artichokes to zucchini, fresh vegetables of some kind are always part of what Italians call il contorno or accompaniments. But this suggests a supporting role, while many of the vegetable dishes in this chapter would make light meals in themselves, or a delicious addition to an antipasto platter.

panzanella

tips add capers for extra flavor.
Instead of discarding the soft white center of the bread, you can blend or process it into fine breadcrumbs, or try cutting it into small cubes and toasting until golden brown and crunchy.

½ loaf stale ciabatta (10oz)
6 medium tomatoes (2lbs 7oz)
2 trimmed sticks celery
1 lebanese cucumber
1 medium red onion

¼ cup (60ml) red wine vinegar
½ cup (125ml) olive oil
1 clove garlic, crushed
¼ cup finely shredded fresh basil

1 Remove and discard soft center from ciabatta; cut remaining bread into 1in cubes.
2 Cut tomatoes into wedges. Discard seeds; chop coarsely.
3 Cut celery into four strips lengthways; chop strips coarsely.
4 Peel cucumber; cut in half lengthways. Discard seeds; cut halves into ¼in-thick slices.
5 Chop onion coarsely; combine with bread cubes, tomato, celery and cucumber in large bowl.
6 Combine remaining ingredients in screw-top jar; shake well. Pour dressing over salad; toss gently.
preparation time 25 minutes   serves 4   per serving   30.1g fat; 381 cal

artichokes with lemon caper dressing

4 medium artichokes (1lb 13oz)
½ cup (125ml) lemon juice
½ cup (125ml) light olive oil

2 cloves garlic, crushed
2 tablespoons capers, chopped coarsely
¼ cup coarsely chopped fresh flat-leaf parsley

1 Trim artichoke stalks to ½in; remove tough outer leaves. Cut off top quarter of remaining leaves. Using small spoon, scoop out center of artichoke to remove choke; discard.
2 Place artichokes, cut-side down, in steamer. Steam artichokes, covered tightly, about 45 minutes or until stems are tender when tested with a skewer; cut in half. Place hot artichokes on serving plates; drizzle with combined remaining ingredients.
preparation time 20 minutes   cooking time 45 minutes   serves 4   per serving   30g fat; 310 cal

grilled vegetables with balsamic dressing

2 medium green peppers (14oz)
2 medium red peppers (14oz)
2 medium yellow peppers (14oz)
1 large red onion (11oz)
2 medium green zucchini (9oz)
2 medium yellow zucchini (9oz)
6 baby eggplants (13oz)

balsamic dressing
2 tablespoons lemon juice
1 clove garlic, crushed
¼ cup (60ml) olive oil
2 tablespoons balsamic vinegar
1 tablespoon coarsely chopped fresh oregano

store salad is best made a day ahead to infuse grilled vegetables with the flavor of the dressing.

1 Quarter peppers; remove and discard seeds and membranes. Cut into thick strips. Cut onion into eight wedges.

2 Cut zucchini and eggplants lengthways into thin slices.

3 Cook vegetables, in batches, on heated oiled grill plate (or grill or barbecue) until browned all over and tender. Combine vegetables in large bowl. Drizzle with balsamic dressing; mix well.

balsamic dressing combine ingredients in screw-top jar; shake well. [Can be made a week ahead and refrigerated, covered.]

preparation time 15 minutes cooking time 20 minutes serves 6 per serving 10.2g fat; 152 cal

radicchio and fennel salad

1 radicchio lettuce
2 medium fennel bulbs (2lbs 4oz),
    cut into ½in strips
4oz pitted black olives
½ cup firmly packed fresh parsley

dressing
¼ cup (60ml) olive oil
1 tablespoon lemon juice
2 anchovy fillets
3 pitted black olives
1 clove garlic, crushed

1 Separate lettuce leaves; wash thoroughly.
2 Arrange lettuce, fennel, olives and parsley on plate. Spoon dressing over salad.
dressing blend or process ingredients 10 seconds.
preparation time 20 minutes serves 4 per serving 14.5g fat; 198 cal

peperonata

2 medium red peppers (14oz)
2 medium yellow peppers (14oz)
2 medium green peppers (14oz)
2 tablespoons olive oil
3 medium onions (1lb), sliced thinly
2 cloves garlic, crushed
2 large tomatoes (1lb 2oz), pitted,
    chopped coarsely

¼ cup (60ml) dry white wine
½ cup pimiento-stuffed green olives, chopped
    coarsely
1 tablespoon coarsely chopped fresh
    flat-leaf parsley

store recipe can be made 3 days ahead and refrigerated, covered.

1 Halve peppers; remove and discard seeds and membranes. Cut peppers into thin strips.
2 Heat oil in large frying pan; cook onion and garlic, stirring, until onion is soft. Stir in peppers and tomato; simmer, covered, about 30 minutes or until peppers are soft, stirring occasionally.
3 Stir in wine and olives; simmer, uncovered, about 5 minutes or until liquid evaporates. Stir in parsley; serve peperonata hot or cold.
preparation time 15 minutes cooking time 35 minutes serves 6 per serving 6.7g fat; 142 cal

peppers with tomato anchovy filling

2 tablespoons olive oil

1 medium onion, chopped finely

1 clove garlic, crushed

½ small eggplant, chopped finely

1 tablespoon coarsely chopped fresh flat-leaf parsley

1 tablespoon coarsely chopped fresh oregano

2 teaspoons drained capers, chopped coarsely

4 drained anchovy fillets, chopped finely

4 medium tomatoes, chopped finely

¼ cup stale breadcrumbs

¼ cup grated parmesan cheese

2 medium red peppers

tip recipe can be prepared a day ahead and refrigerated, covered.

1 Heat half of the oil in large saucepan; cook onion and garlic, stirring, until onion is soft. Stir in eggplant, herbs, capers, anchovy and tomato; cook, stirring, 3 minutes. Transfer mixture to large bowl; cool.

2 Stir in breadcrumbs and cheese.

3 Cut peppers in half lengthways; remove seeds and membranes. Brush skin with remaining oil; place pepper on oven tray. Fill pepper with tomato mixture; bake, uncovered, at 350° F for about 40 minutes or until peppers are tender.

preparation time 20 minutes cooking time 45 minutes serves 4 per serving 11.6g fat; 172 cal

baby rocket and parmesan salad

2oz parmesan cheese

7oz baby rocket

3oz semi-dried tomatoes, halved lengthways

¼ cup pine nuts, toasted

¼ cup (60ml) balsamic vinegar

¼ cup (60ml) extra virgin olive oil

1 Using vegetable peeler, shave cheese into wide, long pieces.

2 Combine rocket with tomato and nuts in large bowl; add cheese. Drizzle with combined vinegar and oil; toss gently.

preparation time 25 minutes   cooking time 3 minutes   serves 8   per serving   16g fat; 177 cal

roasted tomato and cannellini bean salad

2 cups (14oz) dried cannellini beans

6 large tomatoes (1lb 3oz), quartered

⅓ cup (80ml) olive oil

½ teaspoon cracked black pepper

1 tablespoon finely grated lemon rind

¼ cup whole fresh basil

1¾ cups pitted black olives, halved

1 clove garlic, crushed

⅓ cup (80ml) lemon juice

1 teaspoon sugar

tip 2lbs 11oz of any canned white beans, drained and rinsed, can be substituted for dried cannellini beans in this recipe.

1 Cover beans with cold water in large bowl. Soak overnight; drain.

2 Cook beans, uncovered, in large saucepan of boiling water, about 45 minutes or until tender. Drain; cool.

3 Meanwhile, place tomato in large baking dish. Drizzle with half of the oil; sprinkle with pepper. Bake, uncovered, at 475° F for about 30 minutes or until soft.

4 Place beans and tomato in large bowl with rind, basil, olives and remaining ingredients; toss gently to combine.

preparation time 15 minutes (plus soaking time)   cooking time 45 minutes   serves 8
per serving   12g fat; 250 cal

cheese

gorgonzola fritters

Combine 1 cup ricotta cheese, 1 cup coarsely chopped gorgonzola cheese and 2 lightly beaten eggs in medium bowl. Whisk in ½ cup plain flour; stand at room temperature 1 hour. [Can be made a day ahead to this stage and refrigerated, covered.] One-third fill large saucepan with vegetable oil; heat and deep-fry heaped teaspoons of mixture, turning occasionally, until fritters are browned lightly all over and cooked through. Do not have oil too hot or fritters will over-brown before cooking through. Place 1 cup finely grated parmesan cheese in medium bowl; toss fritters, in batches, to coat as they are cooked.

preparation time 15 minutes (plus standing time)
cooking time 5 minutes makes 36
per serving 4g fat; 55 cal

tip gorgonzola is a creamy blue cheese from Italy; if unavailable use blue castello or a similar soft blue cheese.

herbed baked ricotta

Grease deep 8in-round cake pan; line base with baking paper. Place 2lbs 4oz ricotta cheese in large bowl with 2 cloves crushed garlic, 2 lightly beaten eggs, 2 tablespoons finely chopped fresh thyme, 1 tablespoon finely chopped fresh garlic chives and 1 tablespoon finely grated lemon rind; stir until well combined. Spoon cheese mixture into prepared pan. Bake, uncovered, at 350º F for 1 hour or until browned lightly and firm to touch; cool in pan.

preparation time 15 minutes
cooking time 1 hour (plus cooling time)
serves 8 per serving 35.7g fat; 463 cal

marinated bocconcini

Combine 1lb 2oz quartered bocconcini cheese, 6 whole black peppercorns, 3 bay leaves, 3 sprigs fresh rosemary and 3 sprigs fresh oregano in large bowl. Transfer to large sterilized 4-cup jar. Pour ¼ cup white wine vinegar over cheese mixture in jar. Add about 2 cups olive oil, or enough to cover completely; seal. Refrigerate at least 6 hours.

preparation time 5 minutes serves 6
per serving 23.6g fat; 268 cal

tip marinated bocconcini makes a great addition to antipasto platters or fresh green salads; use baby bocconcini, if available.

store recipe can be refrigerated 2 weeks.

parmesan crisps

Combine 1 cup finely grated parmesan cheese, ¼ teaspoon finely ground black pepper and 1 teaspoon dired oregano in medium bowl. Place 2 teaspoons of mixture, 1¼in apart, on baking paper-lined oven trays; flatten with fingertips. Bake, uncovered, in moderately hot oven 4 minutes; cool on trays.

preparation time 5 minutes cooking time 25 minutes makes 18 per serving 1.4g fat; 20 cal

tip although these crisps make a great snack on their own, you can also use them to accompany dips or soup. Make crisps in two large sheets, then break into shards to serve. The flavorings can be omitted and the plain crisps topped with olive paste and a little sour cream for finger food.

store crisps can be made 3 days ahead and stored in an airtight container.

desserts

While the preferred finish to an Italian meal is fruit, when a special occasion demands a special dessert, Italians can produce the most luscious, creamy concoctions imaginable, as well as refreshing fruit-based granita and gelato.

zabaglione

5 egg yolks
¼ cup caster sugar
½ cup (125ml) sweet marsala
¼ cup (60ml) dry white wine

tip zabaglione makes an excellent topping for fresh fruit.

1 Beat yolks and sugar in medium heatproof bowl with electric mixer until well combined.

2 Place bowl of mixture over medium saucepan of simmering water. Gradually beat in half of the marsala and half of the white wine; beat well. Gradually beat in remaining marsala and wine.

3 Beat constantly, about 10 minutes, or until thick and creamy. If mixture adheres to side of bowl, quickly remove from heat and beat vigorously with wooden spoon—especially around base. Pour into individual dishes; serve immediately.

preparation time 10 minutes cooking time 10 minutes serves 4 per serving 7.7g fat; 276 cal

lemon gelato

½ cup caster sugar
½ cup (125ml) water
½ cup (125ml) sweet or dry white wine
½ cup (125ml) lemon juice, strained
1 egg white

store gelato is best made a day ahead and can be frozen, covered for up to 3 days.

1 Combine sugar, the water and wine in small saucepan; stir over low heat until sugar dissolves. Bring to a boil; reduce heat. Simmer, uncovered, 10 minutes; cool. Stir in juice; mix well. Pour into lamington pan; freeze, covered, until mixture is just firm.

2 Remove from freezer. Turn mixture into medium bowl; beat until smooth with fork. Beat egg white in small bowl with electric mixer until firm; fold into lemon mixture. Return to pan; freeze until firm.

preparation time 15 minutes (plus freezing time) cooking time 15 minutes (plus cooling time) serves 2 per serving 0.13g fat; 275 cal

fresh fig and mascarpone tartlets

1 cup flour

1 tablespoon custard powder

1 tablespoon caster sugar

4oz butter, chopped coarsely

1 egg yolk

1 teaspoon grated orange rind

2 teaspoons water, approximately

2 large fresh figs

toffee

1¼ cups caster sugar

½ cup (125ml) water

¼ cup blanched almonds, toasted

½ cup (125ml) strained orange juice

2 tablespoons water, extra

mascarpone cream

½ cup (125ml) thickened cream

7oz mascarpone cheese

1 Grease four deep 4in-round loose-based flan tins. Place flour, custard powder and sugar into medium bowl; rub in butter. Stir in yolk, rind and enough of the water to mix to a soft dough. Knead dough on floured surface until smooth; refrigerate, covered, 1 hour.

2 Roll pastry between sheets of baking paper until large enough to line prepared tins; lift pastry into tins. Press into sides; trim edges. Place tins on oven tray; prick bases with fork. Cover pastry with baking paper; fill with dried beans or rice. Bake, uncovered, at 350º F for10 minutes. Remove paper and beans. Bake, uncovered, further 10 minutes or until browned lightly; cool. [Can be made 3 days ahead and stored in airtight container.]

3 Halve figs; cut each half into three wedges, ready for dipping in toffee.

4 Place pastry cases on serving plates; fill with mascarpone cream. Top each with toffee-coated fig wedges and toffee strands; pour warm orange syrup around tartlets.

toffee cover three cookie trays with foil. Combine sugar and the water in small saucepan; stir over heat, without boiling, until sugar dissolves. Simmer, uncovered, without stirring, until mixture turns golden brown; remove from heat. Dip fig wedges into toffee; place on one cookie tray to set. Place nuts on another cookie tray; pour over half of the remaining toffee. Stand until set; break almond toffee into pieces, then blend or process until crushed finely. Gently reheat remaining toffee; working quickly, dip fork into pan and drizzle long thin strands of toffee onto remaining cookie tray. Add juice and the extra water to any toffee remaining in pan; simmer about 5 minutes or until mixture is syrupy.

mascarpone cream whip cream in small bowl until firm peaks form; fold in mascarpone, in two batches, then finely crushed almond toffee.

preparation time 35 minutes (plus refrigeration time) cooking time 40 minutes serves 4

per serving 68.2g fat; 817 cal

tiramisu

2 tablespoons instant coffee

1¼ cups (310ml) boiling water

1 cup (250ml) sweet marsala

9oz packet sponge-finger biscuits

½ cup (125ml) thickened cream

⅓ cup icing sugar

2 cups mascarpone cheese

1oz dark chocolate, grated

4oz blueberries

tips as with most desserts containing syrup, the flavor will develop more if made a day ahead and refrigerated, covered. Any type of berries is suitable for this recipe.

1 Dissolve coffee in the water in medium bowl. Stir in ⅔ cup of the marsala; cool. Dip half of the biscuits, one at a time, in coffee mixture; arrange in single layer, in a 10-cup glass dish.

2 Beat cream and sugar in small bowl until soft peaks form; fold in the mascarpone and remaining marsala.

3 Spread half of the cream mixture over biscuits in dish. Dip remaining biscuits in remaining coffee mixture; arrange on top of cream layer. Top biscuit layer with remaining cream mixture; sprinkle with chocolate. Cover; refrigerate several hours. [Can be made 2 days ahead to this stage and refrigerated, covered.]

4 Decorate top with blueberries, just before serving.

preparation time 25 minutes serves 6 per serving 59.5g fat; 864 cal

watermelon granita with gingered pineapple

4lbs 7oz watermelon, chopped coarsely

¾ cup sugar

2 cups (500ml) water

4 egg whites

gingered pineapple

2oz piece fresh ginger, sliced thinly

¼ cup (60ml) green ginger wine

½ cup sugar

3 cups (750ml) water

1 small pineapple, chopped coarsely

1 tablespoon finely chopped fresh mint

tip honeydew melon can be substituted for the watermelon.

store recipe must be made several hours before serving.

1 Blend or process watermelon until puréed; push through sieve into large bowl. Discard seeds and pulp; reserve juice.

2 Combine sugar and the water in medium saucepan; stir over low heat until sugar dissolves. Bring to a boil; reduce heat. Simmer, uncovered, without stirring, 10 minutes; cool.

3 Pour sugar syrup into bowl with watermelon juice; stir to combine. Pour granita mixture into 8in x 12oz lamington pan. Cover with foil; freeze about 3 hours or until just set.

4 Remove granita mixture from freezer and place in large bowl with egg whites; beat with electric mixer until smooth. Pour into 5½in x 8in loaf pan. Cover; freeze overnight or until frozen.

5 Serve granita with gingered pineapple.

gingered pineapple combine ginger, wine, sugar and the water in large saucepan; stir over low heat until sugar dissolves. Bring to a boil; reduce heat. Simmer, uncovered, without stirring, 10 minutes. Pour syrup into large heatproof bowl. Add pineapple; cool. Cover; refrigerate 3 hours. [Can be made a day ahead to this stage.] Just before serving, stir in mint.

preparation time 30 minutes cooking time 30 minutes (plus cooling, freezing and refrigeration time)

serves 6 per serving 0.5g fat; 270 cal

ricotta cake

chocolate cake mix

7oz ricotta cheese

¼ cup caster sugar

2 tablespoons Grand Marnier

1oz glacé ginger, chopped finely

1oz glacé cherries, chopped finely

1oz dark chocolate, chopped finely

3oz flaked almonds, toasted

syrup

2 tablespoons caster sugar

⅓ cup (80ml) water

2 tablespoons Grand Marnier

icing

¼ cup caster sugar

⅓ cup (80ml) water

4oz butter

3oz dark chocolate, melted

tip ricotta cake is best made a day ahead and can be refrigerated, covered, 3 days.

1 Make cake mix according to directions on packet; spoon mixture into greased 9in-round cake pan. Bake at 350º F for about 25 minutes or until cake is cooked when tested; turn onto wire rack to cool.

2 Push cheese through wire sieve into small bowl; beat with electric mixer until smooth and creamy. With motor operating, gradually beat in sugar and Grand Marnier, beating well between additions. Stir in ginger, cherries and chocolate; mix well.

3 Cut cake horizontally into three layers. Place one layer on serving plate; brush with syrup.

4 Spread half of the ricotta mixture over cake. Top with second layer of cake; brush with syrup. Spread with remaining ricotta mixture. Top with remaining layer of cake; brush with syrup.

5 Spread icing over top and side of cake; press nuts around side of cake. Refrigerate until ready to serve; stand at room temperature 10 minutes before serving. Cut into wedges to serve.

syrup combine sugar, the water and Grand Marnier in small saucepan. Stir over low heat until sugar dissolves; allow to cool.

icing place sugar and the water in small saucepan. Stir over low heat until sugar dissolves; bring to a boil. Remove from heat; cool. Beat butter until soft and creamy; gradually beat in cooled syrup, a few drops at a time. Gradually add chocolate to butter mixture; beat until well combined.

preparation time 1 hour cooking time 1 hour (plus cooling time) serves 8 per serving 31.3g fat; 576 cal

panettone custards with macadamia toffee

1lb 2oz panettone

2oz softened butter

3½ cups (875ml) milk

1 vanilla bean, halved lengthways

4 eggs

1 cup sugar

¾ cup macadamias, chopped coarsely

2 tablespoons water

2 teaspoons icing sugar

tip brioche, hot cross buns or fruit loaf can be substituted for the panettone.

1 Grease six 1-cup ovenproof dishes.

2 Cut panettone into ½in-thick rounds; spread one side of each round with butter. Cut each round into quarters; divide among prepared dishes.

3 Combine milk and vanilla bean in medium saucepan; bring almost to a boil. Remove from heat; stand, covered, 10 minutes.

4 Meanwhile, whisk eggs and half of the sugar in large heatproof jug. Gradually whisk hot milk mixture into egg mixture. Strain into large jug; discard vanilla bean.

5 Carefully pour egg mixture over panettone in prepared dishes. Place dishes in large baking dish; add enough boiling water to come halfway up sides of dishes. Bake, uncovered, at 325º F for about 30 minutes or until set.

6 Meanwhile, place nuts on oven tray; toast, uncovered, in oven with panettone about 10 minutes or until browned lightly. Place remaining sugar and the water in small saucepan; stir over heat, without boiling, until sugar dissolves. Boil, uncovered, without stirring, about 10 minutes or until sugar syrup is golden brown; pour over nuts. Cool; chop toffee coarsely.

7 Serve custards topped with toffee; dust tops lightly with icing sugar.

preparation time 20 minutes cooking time 40 minutes (plus standing time) serves 6

per serving 51.5g fat; 892 cal

zuccotto

8in-round plain sponge cake
2 tablespoons brandy
2 tablespoons maraschino liqueur
3oz dark chocolate
1¼ cups (310ml) cream
¼ cup icing sugar

1 cup blanched almonds, toasted, chopped
  coarsely
½ cup coarsely chopped roasted hazelnuts
1 teaspoon cocoa powder
1 teaspoon icing sugar, extra

store zuccotto is best made
a day ahead and can be
refrigerated, covered, 3 days.

1 Line 5-cup pudding bowl with a layer of damp muslin.

2 Cut cake into ½in-thick slices. Cut each slice, diagonally, making two triangular sections.

3 Place cake around inside edge of prepared bowl, making sure narrowest end of cake is in the base of
bowl; fill any gaps with pieces of cake. Trim edge; reserve any cake pieces.

4 Combine brandy and maraschino in small jug. Carefully brush cake with brandy mixture.

5 Chop a third of the chocolate finely; reserve. Melt remaining chocolate. Beat cream and sifted icing
sugar in small bowl with electric mixer until firm peaks form; fold in nuts. Halve cream mixture. Fold
chopped chocolate through one half; fold melted chocolate through remaining half. Spoon chopped
chocolate mixture evenly over entire cake surface, leaving a cavity in center; spoon remaining chocolate
mixture into cavity.

6 Arrange reserved cake pieces over filling; brush with any remaining brandy mixture. Cover; refrigerate
overnight. [Can be made 2 days ahead to this stage.]

7 Turn carefully onto serving plate; remove muslin. Dust top with combined cocoa and extra icing sugar.

preparation time 1 hour (plus refrigerating time) cooking time 5 minutes serves 6
per serving 52.8g fat; 973 cal

cassata

2 eggs, separated
½ cup icing sugar
½ cup (125ml) cream
few drops almond essence
chocolate layer
2 eggs, separated
½ cup icing sugar
½ cup (125ml) cream, beaten lightly
2oz dark chocolate, melted
2 tablespoons cocoa powder
1½ tablespoons water

fruit layer
1 cup (250ml) cream
1 teaspoon vanilla essence
1 egg white, beaten lightly
⅓ cup icing sugar
2 tablespoons finely chopped red glacé cherries
2 glacé apricots, chopped finely
2 glacé pineapple rings, chopped finely
1 tablespoon finely chopped green
glacé cherries
⅓ cup flaked almonds, toasted

store cassata is best made a day ahead and can be frozen, covered, 3 days.

1 Beat egg whites in small bowl with electric mixer until firm peaks form; gradually beat in sifted icing sugar. Fold in lightly beaten egg yolks. Beat cream and essence in small bowl with electric mixer until soft peaks form; fold into egg mixture. Pour into deep 8in-round springform cake pan. Smooth over top; freeze, covered, until firm.
2 Spread chocolate layer over almond layer; freeze, covered, until firm.
3 Spread fruit layer over chocolate layer; freeze, covered, until firm.
4 Run small spatula around edge of cassata; wipe a hot cloth over base and side of pan. Turn cassata onto serving plate; cut into wedges to serve. Sprinkle with extra glacé cherries, if desired.
chocolate layer beat egg whites in small bowl with electric mixer until firm peaks form; gradually beat in sifted icing sugar. Beat cream in small bowl until soft peaks form; fold in egg white mixture. Place chocolate in small bowl; stir in egg yolks. Combine cocoa and the water in small jug; stir into chocolate mixture. Fold chocolate mixture through cream mixture.
fruit layer beat cream and essence in small bowl with electric mixer until firm peaks form. Beat egg whites in small bowl with electric mixer until firm peaks form; gradually beat in sifted icing sugar. Fold egg white mixture into cream; gently stir through fruit and nuts.
preparation time 1 hour (plus freezing time) serves 8 per serving 34.6g fat; 480 cal

chocolate cannoli

1½ cups flour

2 tablespoons cocoa powder

2 egg yolks

1 egg, beaten lightly

2 tablespoons coffee-flavored liqueur

1 tablespoon olive oil

1½ tablespoons water, approximately

flour, extra

1 egg white

vegetable oil for deep-frying

16 strawberries

ricotta filling

5 cups ricotta cheese

½ cup icing sugar

1⅓ cups white chocolate melts, melted

⅓ cup (80ml) coffee-flavored liqueur

chocolate sauce

⅔ cup (160ml) cream

4oz dark chocolate, chopped coarsely

tip cannelloni pasta shells make excellent cannoli molds; they must be discarded after deep-frying. Metal cannoli molds are available at specialty kitchen shops. If you use metal cannoli molds, you're ensured of getting a sufficient number of molds to make this recipe. You can substitute plain ready-made cannoli shells in this recipe.

1 Process flour, cocoa, yolks, egg, liqueur and olive oil with enough of the water to form a soft dough; process until mixture forms a ball. Knead dough on floured surface about 5 minutes or until smooth. Wrap in plastic wrap; refrigerate 1 hour.

2 Divide dough into two portions. Roll each portion through pasta machine set on thickest setting. Fold dough in half; roll through machine, dusting with a little extra flour when necessary. Keep rolling dough through machine, adjusting setting so dough becomes thinner with each roll. Roll to second thinnest setting. Cut dough into 9in x 4in-squares. Ensure each piece is ¼in short of the ends of the pieces of pasta or metal molds.

3 Place whichever mold (see tip) you're using on end of each square.

4 Roll dough around mold; brush overlapping end with a little egg white. Make sure egg white does not touch the mold; press firmly to seal. Repeat with remaining squares.

5 Heat vegetable oil in large saucepan. Deep-fry cannoli, in batches, until crisp; drain on absorbent paper. Carefully remove warm cannoli shells from molds; cool. [Can be made a day ahead to this stage and stored in airtight container.]

6 Spoon ricotta filling into large piping bag fitted with plain ½in tube; pipe ricotta filling into cannoli. Serve chocolate cannoli with chocolate sauce and strawberries.

ricotta filling beat cheese and icing sugar in large bowl with electric mixer until smooth; beat in cooled chocolate and liqueur. [Can be made a day ahead and refrigerated, covered.]

chocolate sauce combine cream and chocolate in small saucepan, stir over low heat until chocolate melts.

preparation time 1 hour (plus refrigeration time) cooking time 25 minutes serves 8

per serving 43.1g fat; 745 cal

zuppa inglese

6 eggs, beaten lightly
1¼ cups caster sugar
1 cup flour
½ cup cornstarch
1½ teaspoons baking powder
⅔ cup (160ml) milk
2 tablespoons rum
1lb 2oz strawberries
7oz blueberries
7oz raspberries
2 teaspoons icing sugar

custard filling
½ cup cornstarch
½ cup custard powder
½ cup caster sugar
2⅓ cups (580ml) milk
2 teaspoons vanilla essence
1⅓ cup (300ml) thickened cream
1oz butter
2 egg yolks

store zuppa inglese is best made a day ahead and can be refrigerated, covered, for 3 days.

1 Beat eggs in medium bowl with electric mixer until thick and creamy. Gradually add sugar; beat until sugar dissolves. Gently fold in flour, cornstarch and baking powder. Pour mixture into greased deep 11in-round cake pan. Bake, uncovered, at 350º F for about 35 minutes or until cake is cooked when tested; turn onto wire rack to cool. Wash and dry cake pan.

2 Split cake, horizontally, into three even layers. Place first layer of cake in clean deep 11in-round cake pan. Brush cake with combined milk and rum. Spread half of the custard filling evenly over cake. Reserve eight strawberries for decorating top of cake; hull and slice remaining strawberries. Sprinkle half of the sliced strawberries over custard layer. Place second layer of cake on top of strawberries; brush with rum mixture. Spread remaining custard filling evenly over cake; sprinkle with remaining strawberries. Top with third layer of cake; brush with remaining rum mixture. Refrigerate, covered, several hours. [Can be made 2 days ahead to this stage.]

3 Turn cake onto serving plate. Decorate top of cake with reserved strawberries, blueberries and raspberries; dust top with sifted icing sugar.

custard filling combine cornstarch, custard powder and sugar in large saucepan. Gradually add milk; stir until smooth. Add essence and cream; stir until combined. Stir over low heat until custard boils and thickens; add butter. Simmer, uncovered, 3 minutes, stirring constantly; remove pan from heat. Add yolks; mix well. Transfer custard to medium heatproof bowl; cover surface with plastic wrap. Allow to become cold; beat well.

preparation time 1 hour (plus refrigerating time) cooking time 50 minutes (plus cooling time) serves 12 per serving 41.1g fat; 670 cal

raspberry hazelnut cake

9oz butter, softened

2 cups caster sugar

6 eggs

1 cup flour

½ cup self-raising flour

1 cup hazelnut meal

⅔ cup (160g) sour cream

11oz fresh or frozen raspberries

mascarpone cream

9oz mascarpone cheese

¼ cup icing sugar mixture

2 tablespoons frangelico

½ cup sour cream

½ cup roasted hazelnuts, chopped finely

tips don't thaw frozen raspberries, as they are less likely to 'bleed' into the cake mixture; any similar-sized berries can be substituted for the raspberries.
Any nut, such as almonds or pecans, can be substituted for the hazelnut meal; blend or process whole roasted nuts until ground finely.

store unfrosted cake can be kept in airtight container at room temperature 3 days, or frozen for up to 3 months; cake can be frosted a day ahead and refrigerated.

1 Position oven shelves; preheat oven to 350º F. Grease deep 9in-round cake pan; line base and side with baking paper.

2 Beat butter and sugar in medium bowl with electric mixer until light and fluffy; add eggs, one at a time, beating until just combined between additions. Mixture will curdle at this stage, but will come together later.

3 Transfer mixture to large bowl; using wooden spoon, stir in flours, hazelnut meal, sour cream and raspberries. Spread mixture into prepared pan.

4 Bake cake at 350º F for about 1½ hours. Stand cake 10 minutes; turn onto wire rack. Turn top-side up to cool.

5 Place cake on serving plate. Using metal spatula, spread mascarpone cream all over cake.

mascarpone cream combine mascarpone, icing sugar, liqueur and sour cream in medium bowl. Using wooden spoon, stir until smooth; stir in nuts.

preparation time 30 minutes cooking time 1 hour 30 minutes serves 12 per serving 50.6g fat; 717 cal

sicilian cheesecake

great italian food desserts

7oz plain chocolate cookies, crushed finely
3oz butter, melted
½ cup (125ml) cream
2oz dark chocolate, grated coarsely

filling
1lb 6oz ricotta cheese
1 cup icing sugar
1 teaspoon vanilla essence
2 tablespoons crème de cacao
2 tablespoons finely chopped mixed peel
2oz dark chocolate, grated finely

1 Combine cookies and butter in medium bowl; press evenly over base of 8in springform tin. Refrigerate while preparing filling.

2 Spoon filling over cookie base; refrigerate at least 6 hours or overnight.

3 Just before serving, beat cream in small bowl with electric mixer until soft peaks form; spread evenly over top of cake. Sprinkle with chocolate.

filling beat cheese, icing sugar, essence and crème de cacao in large bowl with electric mixer until smooth and fluffy. Add peel and chocolate; mix well.

preparation time 30 minutes (plus refrigerating time) serves 10 per serving 27.4g fat; 432 cal

panna cotta with orange toffee sauce

2½ teaspoons powdered gelatine
¾ cup (180ml) milk
2½ cups cream
⅔ cup caster sugar
1 vanilla bean

orange toffee sauce
⅔ cup caster sugar
¼ cup (60ml) water
½ cup (125ml) orange juice

tip serve with peaches grilled with a sprinkling of brown sugar.

1 Lightly oil six ⅔-cup (160ml) dishes. Sprinkle gelatine over ¼ cup (60ml) of the milk. Combine remaining milk, cream and sugar in medium saucepan. Split vanilla bean; scrape out seeds. Add seeds and bean to cream mixture. Stir mixture over low heat, without boiling, until sugar dissolves; bring almost to a boil (surface of mixture should just quiver, not bubble). Remove from heat; stand, covered, 10 minutes.

2 Return cream mixture to heat until quite hot; but not boiling. Remove from heat. Stir in gelatine mixture; strain into jug. Pour cream mixture into prepared dishes; cool. Cover; refrigerate 3 hours or until set. [Can be made 2 days ahead to this stage.]

3 Just before serving, turn panna cotta onto serving plates; serve with orange toffee sauce. Top with sliced strawberries, if desired.

orange toffee sauce combine sugar and the water in small heavy-based saucepan; stir over low heat, without boiling, until sugar dissolves. Brush any sugar crystals from side of pan with wet pastry brush. Boil, uncovered, without stirring, about 10 minutes or until sugar syrup is golden brown; remove from heat. Stir in juice, taking care as it will splutter fiercely. Stir over low heat, without boiling, until toffee dissolves. Cool to room temperature. [Can be made 2 days ahead and refrigerated, covered.]

preparation time 25 minutes (plus standing time) cooking time 15 minutes serves 6
per serving 44.9g fat; 625 cal

soft grape gelato with nutmeg wafers

3lbs 6oz seedless white grapes, approximately
3 egg whites
¾ cup caster sugar
nutmeg wafers
1 egg white
¼ cup caster sugar
2 tablespoons plain flour
½ teaspoon ground nutmeg
1oz butter, melted
2 teaspoons cocoa powder

tips if seedless white grapes are out of season, simply purchase white grapes and seed them yourself.
The high sugar content of this dessert will ensure the gelato remains soft and will not freeze solid.

1 Discard grape stalks; process grapes until smooth. Push mixture through coarse strainer, pressing firmly to extract as much juice as possible. You need 3¼ cups (810ml) juice. Pour juice into large shallow cake pan. Cover with foil; freeze until just firm.
2 Beat egg whites in small bowl with electric mixer until soft peaks form. Gradually add sugar; beat until dissolved between additions.
3 Transfer frozen juice to large bowl; quickly beat with electric mixer until just smooth. Add egg white mixture; beat until combined and smooth.
4 Return mixture to pan. Cover; freeze until firm. [Can be made 3 days ahead to this stage.]
5 Serve grape gelato with nutmeg wafers.
nutmeg wafers beat egg white in small bowl with electric mixer until soft peaks form. Gradually add sugar; beat until dissolved between additions. Stir in flour and nutmeg, then cooled butter; reserve 2 tablespoons of the egg mixture. Place teaspoons of egg mixture about 4in apart on baking paper-lined cookie trays, allowing four per tray; spread with spatula to about 3in rounds. Combine reserved mixture with cocoa in small bowl; mix well. Spoon mixture into piping bag fitted with small plain tube. Pipe circles onto wafers to represent grapes. Bake, uncovered, at 350º F for about 5 minutes or until wafers are browned lightly. Lift wafers carefully from trays; place over handle of wooden spoon to give irregularly round shapes. Cool on wire racks.
preparation time 30 minutes (plus freezing time) cooking time 25 minutes (plus cooling time) serves 8
per serving 3.4g fat; 265 cal

fruit

poached peaches

Combine 1½ cups sauternes-style dessert wine, 2 cups water, 1 cup caster sugar and 1 strip lemon rind in large saucepan; stir over low heat, without boiling, until sugar dissolves. Add 6 medium washed unpeeled peaches; simmer, uncovered, about 20 minutes or until tender. Remove from heat; cool. Transfer syrup and peaches to glass or china bowl. Cover; refrigerate 3 hours. [Can be made 2 days ahead to this stage.] Peel peaches; discard peel and rind. Serve peaches with some of the syrup.

preparation time 5 minutes (plus refrigeration time) cooking time 25 minutes serves 6 per serving 0.1g fat; 283 cal

tips peaches can be sliced for serving. If you choose peaches with a pink blush, poaching in their skins will intensify the blush on the peeled fruit.

honey grilled figs

Gently break 6 large figs in half lengthways. Place figs on oven tray; sprinkle broken sides of figs with 2 tablespoons caster sugar. Broil about 5 minutes or until sugar melts and figs are browned lightly. Meanwhile, combine ¼ cup honey and 1 teaspoon vanilla essence in small saucepan; stir over low heat, without boiling, until honey is very runny. Serve warm figs drizzled with honey mixture.

preparation time 5 minutes cooking time 5 minutes serves 6 per serving 0.2g fat; 101 cal

tips green or purple figs are suitable for this recipe. Serve with dollops of whipped mascarpone and cream.

frozen grapes

Wash 1lb 2oz green grapes and 1lb 2oz red grapes; remove stems. Cut grapes in half; remove seeds. Combine in large bowl with ¼ cup orange-flavored liqueur. Cover; stand 1 hour. Place grapes, cut-side down, on baking paper-lined freezer trays. Cover; freeze several hours or until firm. Transfer grapes to freezer container. Serve straight from freezer.

preparation time 10 minutes (plus standing and freezing) serves 8 per serving 0.2g fat; 110 cal

store recipe can be made 3 months ahead.

mixed berries with mascarpone

Combine 9oz quartered strawberries, 7oz raspberries, 7oz blueberries, 2 tablespoons raspberry vinegar and ¼ teaspoon finely ground black pepper in large bowl. Cover; refrigerate 1 hour or until well chilled. [Can be made a day ahead to this stage.] Whip ½ cup cream in small bowl until soft peaks form; gently fold in 7oz mascarpone in two batches. [Can be made a day ahead to this stage and refrigerated, covered.] Spoon mascarpone cream onto serving plates. Top with berry mixture, including any juices; dust thickly with sifted icing sugar.

preparation time 10 minutes (plus refrigeration time) serves 6 per serving 28.4g fat; 329 cal

tip use your favourite mixture of berries for this recipe.

cakes & cookies

If you've ever succumbed to the sweets displayed in Italian bakeries, you'll know just how perfect the marriage is between a cup of espresso and those delicious morsels. Here is a selection for you to try at home, including florentines, almond torrone and Italy's two famous festive cakes, panettone and panforte di siena (siena cake).

white chocolate and frangelico truffles

¼ cup (60ml) cream

1oz butter

9oz white chocolate, chopped finely

¼ cup roasted hazelnuts, chopped finely

2 tablespoons frangelico

7oz dark chocolate, melted

4oz white chocolate, melted, extra

1 Place cream, butter and white chocolate in medium saucepan; stir over low heat until chocolate melts. Stir in nuts and liqueur; pour mixture into small bowl. Cover; refrigerate, stirring occasionally, about 1 hour or until mixture thickens but does not set.

2 Roll rounded teaspoons of mixture into balls; refrigerate truffles on tray until firm.

3 Working rapidly, dip truffles in dark chocolate; roll gently in hands to coat evenly. Return truffles to tray.

4 Drizzle truffles with extra white chocolate; refrigerate, uncovered, until chocolate is completely set.

preparation time 35 minutes cooking time 5 minutes (plus refrigeration time) makes 32

per serving 7.3g fat; 118 cal

florentines

¼ cup slivered almonds

¼ cup coarsely chopped walnuts

1 tablespoon mixed peel

1 tablespoon golden raisins

5 glacé cherries

3 pieces glacé ginger

2oz butter, melted

¼ cup caster sugar

1 tablespoon cream

4oz dark chocolate, melted

1 Blend or process nuts, peel, raisins, cherries and ginger until chopped finely; transfer to large bowl.

2 Stir butter and sugar in small saucepan, over low heat, until sugar dissolves; bring to a boil. Boil gently about 1 minute, or until mixture starts to turn light golden; do not stir while boiling or mixture will crystallize. Add butter mixture and cream to fruit and nut mixture; mix well.

3 Spoon heaped teaspoons of the mixture onto greased cookie trays, allowing room between each for spreading. For easy handling, it is best to bake only four at a time.

4 Bake, uncovered, at 350º F for 10 minutes or until golden brown; remove from oven. Using spatula, push each florentine into round shape; allow to cool on trays 1 minute. Carefully lift each florentine from tray onto wire cooling rack; allow to cool.

5 Spoon 1 teaspoon of the chocolate onto flat side of each florentine; spread out to edge. When chocolate is almost set, run fork through chocolate to give wavy effect. Place on tray; refrigerate until chocolate is set.

preparation time 40 minutes cooking time 50 minutes (plus cooling time) makes 20

per serving 6.8g fat; 96 cal

225

olive oil cake

3 eggs, beaten lightly
1 cup caster sugar
1 tablespoon grated orange rind
2¼ cups self-raising flour
¼ cup (60ml) orange juice
½ cup (125ml) skim milk
1 cup (250ml) extra virgin olive oil
½ cup (125ml) orange juice, warmed, extra
¼ cup icing sugar

tip lemon rind and juice can be substituted for the orange.

1 Oil deep 9in-square cake pan.

2 Beat egg, sugar and rind in medium bowl with electric mixer until very thick and creamy and sugar dissolves. Stir in flour, then combined juice, milk and oil in three batches. Pour mixture into prepared pan.

3 Bake at 400° F for about 45 minutes or until cooked when tested. Stand cake in pan 5 minutes; turn onto wire rack placed over tray. Turn cake again so it is right-side up.

4 Pour extra juice over hot cake; sift icing sugar over top of juice. Cool before serving.

preparation time 25 minutes cooking time 45 minutes (plus standing time) serves 10
per serving 24.8g fat; 445 cal

fig and nut cake

3 eggs

½ cup caster sugar

4oz roasted hazelnuts, chopped coarsely

3oz slivered almonds, chopped coarsely

4oz dried figs, chopped coarsely

4oz mixed peel, chopped coarsely

3oz dark chocolate, chopped finely

1¼ cups self-raising flour

tip fig and nut cake is best made a day ahead. Can be stored in airtight container, 3 days.

1 Beat eggs and sugar in medium bowl with electric mixer until light and fluffy. Transfer to large bowl.

2 Add nuts, fig, peel and chocolate; stir gently until combined.

3 Gently fold sifted flour into mixture. Place mixture into greased 6in x 9in loaf pan; bake at 350° F for about 1 hour or until light golden brown and cooked when tested. Allow to cool slightly in pan; turn onto wire rack to cool completely before cutting.

preparation time 25 minutes cooking time 1 hour (plus cooling time) serves 8

per serving 21.7g fat; 451 cal

almond crunch

1¾ cups caster sugar

2 tablespoons lemon juice

1 cup whole blanched almonds

¼ cup golden syrup

1¼ cups (300ml) cream

store almond crunch can be made 3 days ahead and stored in airtight container in a cool, dry place.

1 Combine ½ cup of the sugar and juice in medium saucepan; stir over low heat, without boiling, until sugar dissolves. Bring to a boil, without stirring, about 6 minutes or until sugar turns dark golden brown. Remove pan from heat. Add almonds; mix well. Drop mixture onto marble slab or oven tray that has been sprinkled with water; cool.

2 Place remaining sugar, golden syrup and cream in large heavy-based saucepan; bring to a boil over moderate heat, stirring. Reduce heat; continue cooking, without stirring, until a little dropped into cold water forms a ball between two fingers (259° F on a sugar (candy) thermometer). This will take about 30 minutes; be careful the mixture does not boil over.

3 Blend or process almond toffee mixture, in batches, until fairly fine.

4 Mix blended toffee into the hot mixture. Pour into well-oiled 8in x 11in rectangular slice pan; cool. Mark out into pieces about 1in square; cut into squares when cold.

preparation time 15 minutes cooking time 50 minutes (plus cooling time) makes 75

per serving 2.3g fat; 41 cal

panettone

½ cup raisins

¼ cup mixed peel

½ cup golden raisins

⅓ cup (80ml) sweet marsala

2 tablespoons dry yeast

1 teaspoon caster sugar

¼ cup (60ml) warm milk

5 cups flour

1 teaspoon salt

¼ cup caster sugar, extra

3 eggs, beaten lightly

3 egg yolks

2 teaspoons grated orange rind

1 teaspoon vanilla essence

4oz butter, softened

1 cup (250ml) warm milk, extra

1 egg, beaten lightly, extra

store recipe can be made 2 days ahead and stored in airtight container.

1 Grease two deep 8in-round cake pans. Using string, tie a collar of greased foil around outside of prepared pans, bringing foil about 2½in above edges of pans.

2 Combine fruit with marsala in small bowl. Cover; stand 30 minutes. Combine yeast, sugar and milk in small bowl; whisk until yeast dissolves. Cover bowl; stand in warm place about 10 minutes or until mixture is frothy.

3 Place flour, salt and extra sugar in large bowl; make well in center. Add eggs and egg yolks, then rind, essence, butter, extra milk, yeast mixture and undrained fruit mixture.

4 Using wooden spoon, beat dough vigorously about 5 minutes (this beating is important). The dough will be soft like cake batter, and will become elastic and leave the side of the bowl. Cover bowl with greased plastic wrap; stand in warm place about 30 minutes or until dough doubles in size. Turn dough onto floured surface; knead about 10 minutes or until smooth. Cut dough in half; knead each half on well-floured surface about 5 minutes or until dough loses its stickiness. Press dough into prepared pans. Cover; stand in warm place about 30 minutes or until dough doubles in size. Brush with extra egg. Bake, uncovered, at 400° F for about 15 minutes. Reduce heat to moderate; bake, uncovered, further 30 minutes. Cool on wire racks.

preparation time 40 minutes (plus standing time) cooking time 45 minutes makes 2
per loaf 71.7g fat; 2591 cal

sicilian creams

1¾ cups self-raising flour
2oz butter
½ cup caster sugar
1 teaspoon grated lemon rind
1 teaspoon vanilla essence
1 egg

¼ cup (60ml) milk
¼ cup (60ml) cream
2 tablespoons icing sugar
1 tablespoon water
1 tablespoon liqueur
1 tablespoon icing sugar, extra

tip sicilian creams are best assembled close to serving. Any liqueur can be used to flavor these cookies, e.g. Grand Marnier, Cointreau or Amaretto.

1 Place flour in large bowl; rub in butter. Add sugar; mix well. Make well in center of mixture; add combined rind, vanilla, egg and milk. Using wooden spoon, mix to a soft, pliable dough.
2 Turn dough onto lightly floured surface; knead gently until smooth. Dough should be soft and pliable.
3 Roll dough out gently until ½in thick. Cut into rounds using 2in cutter; place on lightly greased oven trays, about 1in apart. Bake, uncovered, at 350º F for about 15 minutes or until light golden brown; cool on wire rack. [Can be made 2 days ahead to this stage and refrigerated, covered.]
4 Beat cream and icing sugar in small bowl with electric mixer until firm peaks form. Using fine serrated knife, split each cookie in half, horizontally; brush cut side of each top half of cookie with combined water and liqueur. Join cookies with cream; dust with extra icing sugar.
preparation time 35 minutes cooking time 20 minutes (plus cooling time) makes 12
per serving 7.9g fat; 198 cal

amaretti

1 cup almond meal
1 cup caster sugar
2 large egg whites

½ teaspoon vanilla essence
2 drops almond essence
20 blanched almonds

store amaretti can be made 3 days ahead and stored in airtight container.

1 Beat almond meal, sugar, egg whites and essences in medium bowl with electric mixer, on medium speed, 3 minutes; stand 5 minutes.
2 Spoon mixture into piping bag fitted with ½in plain tube; pipe in circular motion from center, to make cookies about 2in in diameter leaving 1in between each. Top with almonds.
3 Bake, uncovered, in moderate oven, about 12 minutes or until tops are browned lightly. Stand on trays 5 minutes before removing with metal spatula. Cool on wire rack.
preparation time 15 minutes (plus standing time) cooking time 15 minutes makes 20
per serving 4.1g fat; 87 cal

almond torrone

A sugar (candy) thermometer, available from kitchenware stores, is essential for this recipe. Place thermometer in large saucepan of simmering water while syrup is starting to heat. This will stop thermometer cracking when placed in syrup. Once syrup is correct temperature, return thermometer to pan of water; remove from heat. When cool, rinse and dry. You will also need a powerful electric mixer. Choose one on a stand as they generally have more powerful motors than most hand-held electric mixers.

tip this type of rice paper, generally imported from Holland, is whiter than the asian variety and looks more like a grainy sheet of paper.

store torrone can be made a week ahead and stored in airtight container in a cool, dry place.

2 sheets (6in x 8in) rice paper
3 cups blanched almonds
½ cup honey
1⅓ cups caster sugar
2 tablespoons water
1 egg white

1 Preheat oven to 350º F. Lightly grease 3in x 10in bar pan. Line pan with a strip of baking paper, covering base and extending 2in over two long sides. Place one sheet of rice paper in pan, covering base and extending up two long sides.
2 Spread almonds in single layer on oven tray; bake in moderate oven about 10 minutes or until well browned. Transfer to large heatproof bowl. Meanwhile, combine honey, sugar and the water in small saucepan; stir over low heat, without boiling, until sugar dissolves. Using pastry brush dipped in hot water, brush down side of pan to dissolve all sugar crystals.
3 Bring syrup to a boil; boil, uncovered, without stirring, about 10 minutes or until syrup reaches 327º F on sugar (candy) thermometer. Remove immediately from heat. Just before syrup is ready, beat egg white in small heatproof bowl with electric mixer until soft peaks form. With motor operating, add hot syrup to egg white in a thin stream. Beat until all syrup is added.
4 Working quickly, transfer egg white mixture to bowl with almonds; stir until combined. Spoon mixture into prepared pan; press in firmly. Cut remaining sheet of rice paper to fit top of nougat; press on lightly. Stand about 2 hours or until cooled to room temperature. When cooled, transfer to airtight container; do not refrigerate. Cut into ½in slices.
preparation time 15 minutes (plus standing time) cooking time 20 minutes makes 25 slices
per slice 10.6g fat; 182 cal

siena cake

¾ cup blanched almonds, toasted, chopped
  coarsely
1 cup coarsely chopped
  roasted hazelnuts
¼ cup finely chopped glacé apricots
¼ cup finely chopped glacé pineapple
⅓ cup mixed peel, chopped finely

⅔ cup flour
2 tablespoons cocoa powder
1 teaspoon ground cinnamon
⅓ cup caster sugar
½ cup honey
2oz dark chocolate, melted

1 Combine nuts, apricots, pineapple, peel, flour, cocoa and cinnamon in large bowl; mix well.
2 Lightly grease 8in-round sandwich pan. Line base and side with baking paper.
3 Place sugar and honey in medium saucepan; stir over low heat until sugar dissolves, brushing down side of pan to dissolve any sugar crystals. Bring to a boil; reduce heat. Simmer, uncovered, about 5 minutes or until syrup forms a soft ball when a few drops are dropped into a glass of cold water. Add syrup and chocolate to fruit and nut mixture; mix well.
4 Spread mixture quickly and evenly into prepared pan. Bake, uncovered, at 325° F for 35 minutes; cool in pan. Turn out; remove paper. Wrap in foil; leave at least one day before cutting.
preparation time 30 minutes cooking time 1 hour (plus cooling time) serves 8
per serving 21.1g fat; 458 cal

tip siena cake is a perfect accompaniment for after-dinner coffee. Cut into thin wedges or slices about ½in thick, then into small pieces.

store recipe can be made 3 weeks ahead and wrapped tightly in foil.

espresso syrup cake

3 teaspoons instant espresso-style coffee
1 tablespoon hot water
3 eggs, beaten lightly
¾ cup caster sugar
1 cup self-raising flour
1 tablespoon cocoa powder
5oz butter, melted

espresso syrup
¾ cup caster sugar
¾ cup (180ml) water
3 teaspoons instant espresso-style coffee

1 Grease 8in baba pan. Combine coffee and the water in small jug; stir until dissolved.
2 Beat egg in small bowl with electric mixer about 8 minutes or until thick and creamy; gradually add sugar, beating until dissolved between additions. Fold in sifted flour and cocoa, then butter and coffee mixture; pour mixture into prepared pan.
3 Bake, uncovered, at 350° F for about 40 minutes. Stand cake in pan 5 minutes; turn onto wire rack over tray. Reserve ¼ cup (60ml) espresso syrup; drizzle remaining hot syrup over hot cake. Serve with reserved syrup.
espresso syrup combine ingredients in small saucepan; stir over heat, without boiling, until sugar dissolves. Bring to a boil; transfer to heatproof jug.
preparation time 20 minutes cooking time 45 minutes serves 8 per serving 17.7g fat; 387 cal

store recipe can be made 3 days ahead and stored in airtight container.

biscotti

store biscotti can be stored in airtight container 2 weeks.

lemon and pistachio

Beat 2oz coarsely chopped butter, 1 cup caster sugar, 1 teaspoon vanilla essence and 1 tablespoon finely grated lemon rind in medium bowl until just combined. Add 3 eggs, one at a time, beating until combined between additions. Stir in 2¼ cups flour, 1 teaspoon baking powder, ½ teaspoon baking soda and 1 cup coarsely chopped shelled pistachios. Cover; refrigerate 1 hour. Knead dough on lightly floured surface until smooth but still sticky. Halve dough; shape each half into a 12in log. Place each log on greased oven tray. Combine 1 egg and 1 tablespoon water, brush mixture over logs; sprinkle thickly with 2 tablespoons caster sugar. Bake at 350º F for 20 minutes or until firm; cool on trays. Using serrated knife, cut logs, diagonally, into ½in slices. Place slices on ungreased cookie trays. Bake at 325º F for 15 minutes or until dry and crisp, turning halfway through; cool on wire racks.

preparation time 20 minutes (plus refrigeration time) cooking time 40 minutes (plus cooling time) makes 60 per biscotti 2.5g fat; 62 cal

coffee and hazelnut

Whisk ½ cup caster sugar and 1 egg together in medium bowl; stir in ¾ cup flour, ½ teaspoon baking powder and 1 tablespoon espresso-style instant coffee. Stir in 1 cup coarsely chopped toasted hazelnuts; mix to a sticky dough. Using floured hands, roll into an 8in log. Place on greased cookie tray. Bake at 350º F for 25 minutes or until browned lightly and firm; cool on tray. Using a serrated knife, cut log, diagonally, into ½in slices; place on ungreased cookie tray. Bake at 325º F for 15 minutes or until dry and crisp, turning halfway through; cool on wire racks. Spread 4oz melted dark chocolate over one cut side of each biscotti. Allow to set at room temperature.

preparation time 35 minutes (plus setting time) cooking time 40 minutes (plus cooling time) makes 20 per biscotti 6.5g fat; 116 cal

aniseed

Cream 4oz unsalted butter and ¾ cup caster sugar in large bowl; add 3 eggs, one at a time, beating until combined between additions. Add 2 tablespoons brandy and 1 tablespoon grated lemon rind; mix well. Stir in 1½ cups flour, ¾ cup self-raising flour and ½ teaspoon salt. Stir in 4oz coarsely chopped toasted blanched almonds and 1 tablespoon ground aniseed; refrigerate, covered, 1 hour. Halve dough; shape each half into a 12in log. Place on greased cookie tray. Bake at 350º F for 20 minutes or until lightly golden brown; cool on trays. Using serrated knife, cut logs diagonally into ½in slices. Place slices on ungreased cookie trays. Bake at 350º F for 25 minutes or until dry and crisp, turning halfway through cooking; cool on wire racks.

preparation time 40 minutes (plus refrigeration time) cooking time 1 hour (plus cooling time) makes 40 per biscotti 4.9g fat; 95 cal

swirled choc-almond

Beat 2oz butter, 1 cup caster sugar and 1 teaspoon vanilla essence in medium bowl until just combined. Add 3 eggs, one at a time, beating until combined between additions. Stir in 2¼ cups flour, 1 teaspoon baking powder, ½ teaspoon baking soda and 1½ cups coarsely chopped almonds. Cover; refrigerate 1 hour. Halve dough. Knead ¼ cup cocoa powder into one half; shape into a 12in log. Knead ¼ cup flour into remaining dough; shape into a 12in log. Gently twist cocoa log and plain log together; place on greased cookie tray. Bakeat 350º F for 45 minutes or until firm; cool on tray. Using serrated knife cut log, diagonally, into ½in slices. Place slices on ungreased cookie trays. Bake at 325º F for 15 minutes or until dry and crisp, turning halfway; cool on wire racks.

preparation time 25 minutes (plus refrigeration time) cooking time 45 minutes (plus cooling time) makes 25 per biscotti 8.2g fat; 170 cal

glossary

anchovy fillets

artichoke hearts

bortoli beans

dried cannellini

dried haricot

almond

  essence almond extract.

  kernels shelled almonds; brown skin is intact.

  meal finely ground almonds; powdered to a flour-like texture. Used in baking or as a thickening agent.

almonds

  blanched skins removed.

  flaked paper-thin slices.

  slivered small lengthways-cut pieces.

Amaretto an almond-flavored liqueur.

anchovy fillets salted fillets; available rolled or flat and packaged or canned in oil.

aniseed, ground ground leaf of the aniseed myrtle plant.

artichoke

  globe large flower-bud of a member of the thistle family; having tough petal-like leaves, edible in part when cooked.

  hearts tender center of the globe artichoke; sold in cans or loose, in brine.

bacon slices slices of bacon; made from pork side, cured and smoked.

baking powder a raising agent consisting mainly of 2 parts cream of tartar to 1 part baking soda).

basil an aromatic member of the mint family with both culinary and medicinal uses. Many varieties; most commonly used is sweet basil.

bay leaves aromatic leaves from the bay tree; use fresh or dried.

beans

  borlotti also known as roman beans; pale pink with dark red spots, eat fresh or dried.

  broad also known as fava beans; available fresh, canned and frozen. Fresh beans are best peeled twice; discard both the outer long green pod and the sandy-green tough inner shell.

  dried cannellini small, dried white bean similar in appearance and flavor to great northern and navy or haricot beans.

  dried haricot small, dried white bean similar in appearance and flavor to other phaseolus vulgaris, great northern, navy and cannelloni beans.

beef

  eye-fillet tenderloin.

  rump steak boneless tender cut.

  sirloin steaks good-quality steak with t-bone or boneless; new york-style steak.

bicarbonate of soda also known as baking soda.

blue swimmer crabs also known as sand crabs; Atlantic blue crabs.

brandy spirit distilled from wine.

breadcrumbs

  packaged fine-textured, crunchy, purchased, white breadcrumbs; will keep almost indefinitely, in an airtight container.

  stale also known as soft breadcrumbs; 1- or 2-day old bread made into crumbs by grating, blending or processing. Can be frozen for up to 6 months.

butter use salted or unsalted ('sweet') butter; 4oz is equal to 1 stick butter.

buttermilk low-fat milk cultured to give a slightly sour, tangy taste; low-fat yogurt can be substituted.

calamari a type of mollusc; also known as squid. Slice hood thinly to form rings.

calves liver available from butchers; remove silvery membrane after rinsing.

capers gray-green buds of a warm climate (usually Mediterranean) shrub, sold either dried and salted or pickled in a vinegar brine. The smaller capers are better.

cardamom available in pod, seed or ground form with a distinctive aromatic, sweetly rich flavor. Native to India, it's one of the world's most expensive spices.

cashews we used unsalted roasted cashews in this book.

chicken

  breast fillets breast halved, skinned and boned.

  drumsticks leg with skin intact.

  ground finely ground fresh chicken.

  tenderloins thin strip of meat lying just under the breast; especially good for stir-fry cooking.

  thigh cutlets thigh with skin and center bone intact; also known as a chicken chop.

chili

  dried, flakes crushed dried chilies.

  powder made from ground chillies; the Asian variety is the hottest. It can be used as a substitute for fresh chillies in the proportion of ½ teaspoon ground chili powder to one medium chopped fresh chili.

  Thai small, medium hot and bright-red to dark-green in color.

chives related to the onion and leek, with a subtle onion flavor.

  garlic have flat leaves and a stronger flavor than chives.

chocolate

  bits also known as chocolate chips; available in milk, white and dark varieties. Made of cocoa liquor, cocoa butter, sugar and an emulsifier, these hold their shape in baking and are ideal for decorating.

  dark eating chocolate; made of cocoa liquor, cocoa butter and sugar.

  drinking powder sweetened cocoa powder.

chocolate-flavored liqueur crème de cacao.

cilantro also called coriander or Chinese parsley; bright-green-leafed herb with a pungent flavor.

  seeds grind seeds after briefly dry-roasting to maintain vibrancy; do not substitute for fresh cilantro.

cinnamon sticks dried inner bark of the shoots of the cinnamon tree. Also available in ground form.

clams we used a small ridge-shelled variety of this bivalve mollusc; also known as vongole.

cloves dried flower buds of a tropical tree; can be used whole or in ground form.

cocoa powder ground cocoa

blue swimmer crab

capers

baby capers

clams

eggplant

fennel

radicchio

beans with half of the butter removed.

coffee-flavored liqueur Tia Maria, Kahlua.

cooking-oil spray vegetable oil in an aerosol can; available in supermarkets.

coriander *see* cilantro.

seeds grind seeds after briefly dry-roasting to maintain vibrancy; do not substitute for fresh cilantro.

cornstarch also known as cornflour; used as a thickening agent in cooking.

cream we used fresh cream in this book, unless otherwise stated. Also known as pure cream and pouring cream; has no additives unlike commercially thickened cream. Minimum fat content 35%.

sour a thick commercially cultured soured cream good for dips, toppings and baked cheesecakes. minimum fat content 35%.

thickened a whipping cream containing a thickener. Minimum fat content 35%.

curly endive also known as frisee; a curly-leafed green vegetable, mainly used in salads.

custard powder powdered thickening agent used in custard; contains starch.

dark rum we prefer to use an underproof (not overproof) for a more subtle flavor.

dill tiny green-yellow flowers with light green, feathery leaves.

dry yeast a leavening agent used in breads.

dry mustard available as powder.

duck we used whole ducks.

eggplant also known as aubergine. Depending on age, they may require slicing and salting to reduce bitterness; rinse and dry well before using. Also baby eggplant.

fennel also known as finocchio or anise; can be eaten raw in salads or braised or fried as a vegetable accompaniment.

flour

white plain an all-purpose wheat flour.

self raising plain flour sifted with baking powder in the proportion of 1 cup flour to 2 teaspoons baking powder.

Frangelico hazelnut-flavored liqueur.

Galliano clear yellow-colored Italian liqueur made from an infusion of herbs and flowers.

garlic a bulb contains many cloves that can be crushed, sliced, chopped, or used whole, peeled or unpeeled.

gelatine also known as gelatin; we used powdered gelatine. It is also available in sheet form known as leaf gelatine.

ginger also known as green or root ginger; the thick gnarled root of a tropical plant.

glacé fruit fruit preserved in sugar syrup.

golden syrup a by-product of refined sugarcane; pure maple syrup or honey can be substituted.

Grand Marnier orange-flavored liqueur based on cognac-brandy.

green ginger wine alcoholic sweet wine with the taste of fresh ginger; dry (white) vermouth or syrup from a jar of preserved ginger can be substituted.

ham

leg good quality ham carved off the bone.

shaved very thinly sliced ham.

hazelnuts also known as filberts. plump, grape-sized, rich, sweet nut having a brown skin (removed by rubbing heated nuts together in a tea-towel).

herbs we used dried (not ground) herbs in the ratio of 1 teaspoon dried herbs to 4 teaspoons chopped fresh herbs.

Lebanese cucumber also known as European or burpless cucumber; this variety is long, slender and thin-skinned.

leek a member of the onion family; resembles the green onion but is much larger.

lemon thyme a variety of thyme with a lemony fragrance.

lettuce

oak leaf also known as feville de chene. Available in red and green leaf varieties.

butter a round, dark green lettuce with soft leaves.

cos also known as roma; has crisp elongated leaves.

iceberg a heavy, firm, round lettuce with tightly packed leaves and crisp texture.

radicchio a type of Italian lettuce with dark burgundy leaves.

rocket also known as arugula, rugla and rucola; a peppery-tasting green leaf that can be eaten raw in salads or cooked in soups, risottos, and the like.

macadamias a rich and buttery nut. Store in refrigerator because of high oil content.

makerel slender, silvery fish with a fine, sweet flavor; usually sold whole.

maple-flavored syrup also known as golden or pancake syrup; made from cane sugar and artificial maple flavoring. It is not a substitute for pure maple syrup.

maraschino liqueur a cherry-flavored liqueur.

marsala a sweet fortified wine originally from Sicily.

mayonnaise a paste consisting of oil, egg and vinegar.

milk we used full-cream homogenized milk unless otherwise specified.

evaporated unsweetened canned milk from which water has been extracted by evaporation.

skim we used milk with 0.1% fat content.

mint a tangy, aromatic herb available fresh or dried.

mixed peel candied citrus peel.

mixed spice a blend of ground spices usually consisting of cinnamon, allspice and nutmeg.

mizuna a Japanese green salad leaf with a delicate mustard flavor; used in mesclun.

mushrooms

button small, cultivated white mushrooms having a delicate, subtle flavor.

flat large, soft, flat mushrooms with a rich earthy flavor; sometimes misnamed field mushrooms.

glossary

nutmeg

puy lentils

white
medium-grain

brown
long-grain

white
long-grain

aborio

flat-leaf
parsley

chives

mint

curly
parsley

basil

oregano

coriander

Swiss brown light to dark brown mushrooms with full-bodied flavor. Button or cup mushrooms can be substituted.

mussels purchase from a reliable fish market. Mussels must be tightly closed when bought, indicating they are alive. before cooking, scrub shells with a strong brush and remove 'beards'. Discard any shells that do not open after cooking.

mustard
Dijon a pale brown, distinctively flavored, fairly mild French mustard.
seeded French-style mustard with crushed seeds.

nutmeg the dried nut of an evergreen tree native to Indonesia; available in ground form or you can grate your own with a fine grater.

octopus, baby must be tenderized before being cooked; curled up tentacles are an indication of tenderness.

olive oil mono-unsaturated; made from the pressing of tree-ripened olives. Extra light or light describes the mild flavor, not the fat levels. Extra virgin and virgin are the highest quality olive oils, obtained from the first pressings of the olive.

olives
kalamata a dark olive, preserved in salt and oil; Greek in origin.
small stuffed green olives stuffed with pimento.

onion
red also known as spanish, red Spanish or Bermuda onion; a sweet-flavored, large, purple-red onion.
green also known as scallion or (incorrectly) shallot; an immature onion picked before the bulb has formed, having a long, bright-green edible stalk.

orange-flavored liqueur Grand Marnier.

oregano a member of the mint family; related to but spicier than marjoram.

panettone an italian cake, containing dried fruit and nuts.

parsley
curly most familiar variety with bright-green, tightly curled leaves.
flat-leaf also known as Continental parsley or Italian parsley.

passion fruit also known as granadilla; a small tropical fruit, native to Brazil, comprised of a tough outer skin encasing edible black sweet-sour seeds.

pear, corella miniature dessert pear with colorful green skin and a gold and red blush; juicy and delicious, it is popular in cheese platters.

pepper also known as bell pepper; available in red, yellow and green varieties. Seeds and membranes should be discarded before use.

peppercorns available in black, white, red or green; we used the black dried variety.

pesto made from garlic, oil, vinegar, pine nuts, basil, herbs and spices. Available bottled from supermarkets.

pine nuts also known as pignoli; small, cream-colored kernels obtained from the cones of different varieties of pine trees.

pistachios pale green, delicately flavored nut inside hard off-white shells. to peel, soak shelled nuts in boiling water about 5 minutes; drain, then pat dry with absorbent paper.

pita also known as lebanese bread or pitta; a wheat-flour pocket bread sold in large, flat pieces separating into two thin rounds.

pizza bases commercially packaged, pre-cooked, wheat-flour round bases.

pork
butterfly steaks skinless, boneless mid-loin chop, split in half and flattened.
rack row of cutlets.

pumpkin also known as squash; we used butternut pumpkin.

puy lentils a very fine, dark blue-green, fast cooking lentil originally from Le Puy in France.

quail a small, delicate flavored, domestically grown game bird, ranging in weight from 8 to 11oz.

rabbit wild rabbit is gamy in flavor with dark colored flesh; farmed rabbit has a more subtle flavor and is paler in color.

rice
arborio small, round-grain rice well-suited to absorb a large amount of liquid; especially suitable for risottos.
brown natural whole grain.
long-grain elongated grain, remains separate when cooked; most popular steaming rice in Asia.
white is hulled and polished; can be short- or long-grained.

rice paper contrary to popular belief, this type of rice paper is made from the pith of a small Asian tree, not rice. The fine, glossy paper is edible and very useful when making biscuits and confectionery.

rolled oats also known as oatmeal or porridge; oat grouts, husked, steamed-softened, flattened with rollers, dried and packaged as a cereal product.

saffron stigma of a member of the crocus family; available in strands or ground form. Imparts a yellow-orange color to food once infused. The most expensive spice in the world; keep refrigerated.

salami
Italian made from pork and red pepper; it is not spicy.
Milano made from pork, garlic, white wine and peppercorns; quite spicy.

salmon red-pink firm-flesh fish with few bones; it has a moist delicate flavor.

sardines small silvery fish with soft, oily flesh.

savoy cabbage large, heavy head with crinkled dark-green outer leaves; a fairly mild tasting cabbage.

scallop a bivalve mollusc with fluted shell valve; we used scallops with the coral (roe) attached.

seafood marinara mix a mixture

italian
milano

scallop

semolina

sponge finger
buscuits

vanilla

vinegars

of uncooked, chopped seafood available from fish markets and fishmongers.

semolina made from durum wheat; milled, various textured granules, all of these finer than flour. The main ingredient in good pastas and some kinds of gnocchi.

sesame seeds black and white are the most common of the tiny oval seeds harvested from the tropical plant sesamum indicum.

smoked haddock white flesh with a milky smoky flavor and an orange skin.

smoked salmon soft, slightly moist flesh with a delicate flavor.

snapper
>*cutlets* thick, cross-ways slices of fish, cut through skin and bones.
>*fillets* tender flesh, cut lengthways.

snow peas also called mange tout ('eat all'). Snow pea tendrils, the growing shoots of the plant, are sold by greengrocers.

spinach correct name for English spinach; the green vegetable often called spinach is correctly known as Swiss chard. Delicate, crinkled green leaves on thin stems; high in iron. Also, baby spinach.

sponge finger biscuits, packet also known as savoiardi, savoy biscuits or ladyfingers; Italian-style, crisp biscuits made from a sponge-cake mixture.

squash also known as patty-pan, scallopine or summer squash; small, flattish yellow or green-skinned squash.

stock 1 cup (250ml) stock is the equivalent of 1 cup (250ml) water plus 1 crumbled stock cube (or 1 teaspoon stock powder).

sugar we used coarse, granulated table sugar, also known as crystal sugar, unless otherwise specified.
>*brown* an extremely soft, fine granulated sugar retaining molasses for its characteristic color and flavor.
>*caster* also known as superfine or finely granulated table sugar.

icing also known as confectioners' sugar or powdered sugar. We used icing sugar mixture, not pure icing sugar.

sugar snap peas small pods with tiny, formed peas inside; they are eaten whole, cooked or uncooked.

Swiss chard also known as silverbeet and mistakenly, spinach; a member of the beet family with tasty green leaves and a celery-like stem.

swordfish steaks an oily firm-fleshed fish.

thyme leaves have a warm, herby taste; can be used fresh or dried.

tomato
>*pasta sauce* bottled prepared sauce available from supermarkets.
>*paste* triple-concentrated tomato purée used to flavor soups, stews, sauces and casseroles.
>*purée* canned puréed tomatoes (not tomato paste). substitute fresh peeled and pureed tomatoes.

tomatoes
>*canned* whole peeled tomatoes in natural juices.
>*cherry* also known as tiny tim or tom thumb tomatoes; small and round.
>*roma* also known as plum or egg, these are smallish, oval-shaped tomatoes much used in italian cooking or salads.
>*sun-dried* we used those bottled in oil, unless otherwise specified.

turmeric, ground a member of the ginger family, its root is dried and ground, giving a rich yellow powder. It is intensely pungent in taste but not hot.

vanilla
>*bean* dried long, thin pod from a tropical golden orchid; the minuscule black seeds inside the bean impart a luscious vanilla flavor in cooking.
>*essence* we used imitation vanilla essence.

veal

>*boned* rolled leg of veal.
>*nut* a lean cut from the leg.
>*schnitzels* thinly sliced steak.
>*shin* also known as osso buco.
>*steaks* schnitzel.

vegetable oil any number of oils sourced from plants rather than animal fats.

vinegar
>*balsamic* a matured Italian vinegar; use sparingly.
>*raspberry* made from fresh raspberries steeped in a white wine vinegar.
>*red wine* based on fermented red wine.
>*sherry* natural vinegar aged in oak, as per the traditional Spanish system.
>*white* made from spirit of cane sugar.
>*white wine* made from white wine.

white fish fillets any non-oily fish; bream, flathead, whiting, snapper, jewfish and ling. Redfish also comes into this category.

witlof also known as chicory or belgian endive.

zucchini also known as courgette; green yellow or gray members of the squash family having edible flowers.

index

conversion chart

MEASURES

The difference between one country's measuring cups and another's is, at most, within a 2 or 3 teaspoon variance, and will not affect your cooking results.
All cup and spoon measurements are level.
The most accurate way of measuring dry ingredients is to weigh them. When measuring liquids, use a clear glass or plastic jug with graduated markings.
We use large eggs with an average weight of 2oz.

DRY MEASURES

IMPERIAL	METRIC
½oz	15g
1oz	30g
2oz	60g
3oz	90g
4oz (¼lb)	125g
5oz	155g
6oz	185g
7oz	220g
8oz (½lb)	250g
9oz	280g
10oz	315g
11oz	345g
12oz (¾lb)	375g
13oz	410g
14oz	440g
15oz	470g
16oz (1lb)	500g
24oz (1½lb)	750g
32oz (2lb)	1kg

LIQUID MEASURES

IMPERIAL	METRIC
1 fluid oz	30ml
2 fluid oz	60ml
3 fluid oz	100ml
4 fluid oz	125ml
5 fluid oz (¼ pint/1 gill)	
	150ml
6 fluid oz	190ml
8 fluid oz	250ml
16 fluid oz (1 pint)	500ml
1 quart	1000ml (1 litre)

LENGTH MEASURES

IMPERIAL	METRIC
⅛in	3mm
¼in	6mm
½in	1cm
¾in	2cm
1in	2.5cm
2in	5cm
2½in	6cm
3in	8cm
4in	10cm
5in	13cm
6in	15cm
7in	18cm
8in	20cm
9in	23cm
10in	25cm
11in	28cm
12in (1ft)	30cm

OVEN TEMPERATURES

These oven temperatures are only a guide for conventional ovens. For fan-forced ovens, check the manufacturer's manual.

	°C (CELSIUS)	°F (FAHRENHEIT)
Very slow	120	250
Slow	150	275-300
Moderately slow	160	325
Moderate	180	350-375
Moderately hot	200	400
Hot	220	425-450
Very hot	240	475

© 2002 by ACP Magazines Ltd

This 2010 edition published by Fall River Press, by arrangement with ACP Magazines Ltd.

Cover Spaghetti puttenesca, page 64
Photographer Rowan Fotheringham
Stylist Jane Hann

Back cover Onion and zucchini frittata, page 178
Photographer Stuart Scott
Stylist Wendy Berecry

Photographers Alan Benson, Kevin Brown, Scott Cameron, Robert Clark, Joe Filshie,
Rowan Fotheringham, Andre Martin, Mark O'Meara, Rob Shaw, Brett Stevens,
Robert Taylor, Jon Waddy

Stylists Lucy Andrews, Clare Bradford, Marie-Helene Clauzon, Jane Collins, Rosemary de Santis,
Georgina Dolling, Carolyn Fienberg, Kay Francis, Jane Hann, Trish Heagerty, Jacqui Hing, Katy Holder,
Cherise Koch, Vicki Liley, Janet Mitchell, Michelle Noerianto, Sarah O'Brien, Anna Phillips, Sophia Young

Fall River Press
122 Fifth Avenue
New York, NY 10011

ISBN: 978-1-4351-2617-6

Printed and bound in China

10 9 8 7 6 5 4 3 2 1